JACCC

Nikkei DONBURI
A Japanese American CULTURAL SURVIVAL GUIDE

WRITTEN BY
Chris Aihara
JAPANESE AMERICAN Cultural & Community Center

Art Direction & Design by **Qris Yamashita** • Illustrations by **Glen Iwasaki**

LIBRARY OF CONGRESS CATALOGING - IN - PUBLICATION DATA

Aihara, Chris, 1950 –
Nikkei Donburi: A Japanese American Cultural Survival Guide
Chris Aihara
p. cm.

Includes bibliographical references (p.115) and Index

Summary
Presents cultural information, stories, activities, and resources related to the Japanese American experience.

ISBN No. 1-879965-18-6
1. Japanese American – Social life and customs – Study and teaching – Activity programs – Juvenile literature.
2. Japanese Americans – Ethnic identity – Study and teaching – Activity programs – Juvenile literature.[1. Japanese Americans – Social life and customs. 2. Japanese Americans – Ethnic identity.]
1.Title

F184.J3A39 1999
390'.089'956073-do21

98-7207
CIP
AC

Japanese American Cultural & Community Center
First Edition, 1999

Text Copyright @ 1999 by Chris Aihara
Illustrations Copyright @ 1999 by Glen Iwasaki

Produced by the Japanese American Cultural & Community Center
Project & Editorial Director Chris Aihara
Art Director/Designer Qris Yamashita
Illustrator Glen Iwasaki

Published by
Polychrome Publishing Corporation
4509 North Francisco Avenue
Chicago, Illinois 606625-3808
(773) 478-4455   Fax (773) 478-0786
http://home.earthlink.net/~polypub/

Printed in Hong Kong
10 9 8 7 6 5 4 3 2 1

ISBN 1-879965-18-6

This book is dedicated to the memory of
JACCC President Toshikazu Terasawa, (1923 – 1995)
a man of generous spirit
who led us by his example
and inspired us to accomplish our best work.

TABLE of Contents

Foreword 6

Introduction 8

Introducing Mia and Ryan **15**

Winter / Fuyu 16

Oshōgatsu Morning **19**

Japanese Oshōgatsu **19**

Issei Generation **23**

Generations **24**

Writing Numbers in Japanese **24**

In Winter, Baachan would...(A Poem) **26**

Itadakimasu & Gochisōsama **28**

Osechi Ryōri: The New Year Feast **29**

Ozōni Recipe **30**

Coloring Winter Foods **31**

Eating Japanese Food **32**

Obāchan's Rules **32**

How to Eat with Hashi **33**

Mochitsuki **34**

Mochi, Mochi, Mochi **34**

New Year Good-luck Charms **36**

Origami Tsuru **37**

Origami Kame **38**

Daruma **39**

Coloring a Daruma **39**

Animal Zodiac **40**

Spring / Haru 42

Hinamatsuri **45**

Origami Hina Doll **48**

Kimono **49**

Designing a Kimono **50**

Proper Bow **51**

Sakura **52**

Sakura (The Song) **52**

Making a Sakura Decoration **53**

The Importance of Being Chanto **54**

Tango no Sekku & Kodomo-no-Hi **57**

Making a Koinobori **58**

Gyotaku **59**

The Story of Momotarō **60**

Momotarō: A Stick Puppet Play **62**

Origami Kabuto **64**

Jan Ken Po **65**

Summer / Natsu 66

Obon: A Gathering of Joy **69**

Getting Ready for Obon **72**

Tankō Bushi (The Song) **73**

Making a Chōchin **74**

Furoshiki **76**

Taiko **77**

Making a Taiko **78**

Nisei Week Japanese Festival **80**

What is Your Favorite Carnival Food? **81**

A Trip to Little Tokyo
Mikawaya, A Japanese Confectionery **82**

Maneki Neko **84**

A Trip to Little Tokyo
Interview with Rev. Kensho Furuya **85**

Musubi **88**

Making a Musubi **89**

Omiyage **90**

Making Wrapping Paper **90**

Tanabata **93**

Haiku **94**

Writing a Haiku **95**

Fall / Aki 96

Grandma's House **98**

My Grandparent's House **99**

Noren **102**

Making a Noren **103**

Tōfu **104**

Mottainai **105**

Japanese Dishes and Kitchen Tools **106**

Tsukemono Recipes **107**

Tsukemono **107**

Enryo **108**

Kanreki **110**

Taking an Oral History **111**

Bibliography 115

Index 117

Acknowledgements 121

JACCC 122

Foreword

The Mission of the Japanese American Cultural and Community Center (JACCC) is to present, perpetuate, transmit and promote Japanese and Japanese American arts and culture to diverse audiences. Our vision is of current and future generations of Japanese Americans who are knowing, engaging, creating, nurturing, validating and passing along cultural traditions, values and arts, as well as integrating them into their daily lives.

The JACCC was established by the Issei and Nisei, and much current work here is carried out by Sansei and Yonsei, exemplified by the recent election of the first Sansei Chair of the JACCC Board of Directors, Judge Kathryn Doi Todd. Sansei are the bridge from the Issei to the Gosei, passing on the spirit and cultural sensibilities of our Issei grandparents to our Gosei grandchildren, continuing the cultural stream that the Issei and Nisei generations worked so hard to establish.

Yet few images, music, designs and textures from our parents and grandparents are maintained in our own lives and homes. Many of us recall a treasured brush painting or even the pattern or texture of Baachan's favorite furoshiki wrap or table runner. I can still hear the music of the *Tankō Bushi* and the smell the teriyaki chicken at the Obon barbecue. How often in our lives today do we see ikebana arrangements or listen to Japanese music?

And if traditional images don't have a place in our lives, have we continued the traditions with contemporary Japanese or Japanese American culture? Do the graphic designs of Ikko Tanaka grace our walls or those of Qris Yamashita our T-Shirts; have we replaced the nagauta with CD's of Hiroshima or Sadao Watanabe? When I think about my own Yonsei children I realize that notwithstanding Panasonic rice cookers and Sony Walkmans, there may be few elements of Japanese or Japanese American culture which they will carry forward into the homes and lives of the Gosei, unless we Sansei give greater support to cultural continuation.

The activities and stories in **Nikkei Donburi** give us an opportunity to retrace some of our paths, to gather information, and to pass that on; to fold origami and cook ozōni for our children and grandchildren just as our parents and grandparents did for us. Once doing that, we also invite you to join us for activities and programs at our Japanese American Cultural and Community Center in Little Tokyo, Los Angeles, or at the the Japanese Cultural and Community Center of Northern California, our partners in this publication, or at any of the many cultural, religious and community institutions which form the basis for our communities.

Our thanks to Chris Aihara, Qris Yamashita, Glen Iwasaki, and the many practitioners of Japanese American culture who participated in this publication. Each day, they practice what this is all about, the survival of our cultural stream in America.

Gerald D. Yoshitomi
Executive Director
Japanese American Cultural & Community Center

Sponsors

Published in cooperation with
The Japanese Cultural & Community Center
of Northern California (JCCCNC)

Nikkei Donburi Sponsors
Japanese American Community Services
In Memory of Toshikazu Tersawa

Japanese American Service Committee of Chicago

Pacific Bell

Henri & Tomoye Takahashi Charitable Foundation

Dedication Contributors (Please see inside covers.)

JACCC Community Programs Supported by:
McDonnell Douglas Foundation
Parsons Foundation

JACCC Programs are made possible in part by grants from the National Endowment for the Arts, California Arts Council, the City of Los Angeles, Cultural Affairs Department, the James Irvine Foundation, Nathan Cummings Foundation, the Union Pacific Foundation and, the Lila Wallace-Reader's Digest Fund.

Our appreciation to our members, donors and patrons whose generous support make possible JACCC events and activities.

Introduction

Nikkei Donburi: A Japanese American Cultural Survival Guide is a mix of stories, things-to-do, cultural information and resources about the Japanese American family. This book has been a project in the works for a long time — beginning 15 years ago with the early years of community programming by the Japanese American Cultural and Community Center (JACCC). Like the Japanese folk hero Momotarō, we were inspired by a noble goal and fueled by youthful confidence, but had no firm plan as to how to *preserve, and present Japanese American culture*. For we are on a continuum, down a road of process begun by Nisei and Issei, each generation of us trodding down "new ground" defining and re-defining as we go along.

Early community programs spilled out via the shot-gun approach, as we scattered ideas, tried and continue to try lots of different things — kids workshops, lectures series, performances, artist-in-residencies... and on and on. From then to now we work with our community — the kids, our *sensei-tachi*, a body of written resources, a network of community organizations — to present programs, and contribute to the growth of Japanese American community culture.

Our family programs provided the resources, raw data and testing ground for a large portion of this book project. The book is subtitled "A Japanese American Cultural Survival Guide" for its impetus was to collect and distribute information that would encourage the continuation of Japanese American cultural activities. I wanted the book to be contemporary, a composite of today's Japanese American lifestyle. I live, work and raise my own family in the Los Angeles area. I debated about depicting Japanese American community life in general, but felt more qualified and comfortable being specific. This may not be everyone's Japanese American experience, but it is one I have observed and experienced. And I feel information in the book and the family life portrayed will make connection with many others. Like a *donburi*, the casual Japanese lunch made up of appetizing combinations of meat, chicken, egg and veggies over rice, this book is a mix of things-to-do, bite-sized entries of information and resources about the Nikkei experience. Donburi is not a static dish; there is room for change and experimentation.

In putting the book together, I chose subject areas relevant to the community life I observe. Some of the activities are derivations of traditional crafts, others obviously are "new spins" on familiar themes. Throughout the book we have tried to support activities and stories with information about their traditional origins. What we hope to encourage is not rote mimicking of tradition, but understanding and internalizing. For example, there is a section in the book on the custom of saying *"itadakimasu"* before eating and *"gochisōsama"* after finishing a meal. Many of us learned these phrases as a child, without knowing their significance. Both phrases underscore appreciation to all persons and living

things who contributed to our meal. In our Japanese American culture, the appreciation of our dependence and reliance on one another is a value we can continue to express.

Structuring and organizing the book was a dilemma. What to include? What to leave out? How to put it all together? I decided to organize around the four seasons to give focus, yet allow for tangents and digressions. Looking at the traditional culture, the response to the changing seasons is obvious in every aspect and detail of Japanese life. This contrasts dramatically with life in Southern California where we have been accused of having no seasons at all. Traditional Japanese associations — smells, colors, sounds, tastes — are different experiences for Japanese Americans, yet key and important cultural activities and celebrations in our community remain connected to specific times in the calendar year, like, Winter and *Oshōgatsu*.

My intent was to make this book "user-friendly," fun, informative and a quick read. It depicts a specific cultural experience, and yet, there are threads of similarity between our stories and the experiences of other ethnic Americans. I hope this publication will communicate to others a clearer picture of the Japanese American experience. Its size was intended to be easy to photo-copy, and therefore, accessible to schools and organizations. Copy the activity pages and keep the book intact. Share the book with a friend.

Nikkei Donburi is the cumulative work of many programs and the resources and talents of many people and organizations. Working on this project has reinforced for me that being connected, contributing and working within a Japanese American community context is how we shall continue and thrive as Japanese Americans. We cannot maintain a culture as single entities and families.

Provided with this opportunity to express my appreciation, I must acknowledge the creativity and talent of the writers who contributed work to this project. I'd like to say thank you to my

JACCC co-workers, who always have enough heart and energy to pursue another "good idea." Special thanks to "the Boss" Jerry Yoshitomi who encourages his staff to extend themselves and take risks. A big thank you to Leslie Ito, and Lori Nakama who helped bring in the finished manuscript. I am grateful to Kats Kunitsugu, Reiko Bissey, Chris Komai, and Gary Kawaguchi for their final edit. Bill Shishima, Mas Matsumoto and Hal Keimi developed and "perfected" many of the children's activities. Thank you to Glen Iwasaki who brings life and sparkle to words on a page. Designer Qris Yamashita takes my copy and creatively moves the project beyond my own vision. My gratitude to my *senpai tachi;* Hiroshi Ito, Lloyd Inui, and Rev. Masao Kodani. Thank you to Sandra Yamate of Polychrome Publishing for her encouragement and advice. And finally, thank you to my extended family of friends, my parents, James and Mary Iwanaga, my brother John, my in-laws Luis and Yae Aihara, and my "more than I deserve" family; Doug, Blair, Garrett, Steve and Riki Aihara.

Chris Aihara, 1998

13

Introducing **Mia and Ryan...**

Five year-old Mia Kimiko and her nine year-old brother Ryan Makoto are *Nikkei,* or of Japanese heritage, and live in a suburb of Los Angeles, California. Mia and Ryan are *Yonsei,* fourth generation Japanese American. Their great-grandparents were born in Japan and immigrated to the United States as young adults. We refer to this first generation of pioneers from Japan as *Issei.*

Mia and Ryan remember their *hi-obāchan* (great-grandmother) on their mom's side who always made the *saba-zushi* or mackerel sushi for holiday parties. They could not speak to her in Japanese, but she always had a big smile and hug for them, (and a little pocket money) whenever they visited.

Most of Mia and Ryan's relatives live nearby. They all get together for the holidays and special occasions. The children visit both their maternal and paternal *Nisei* (second generation) grandparents often. Both of their Nisei grandparents have lived in Southern California all of their lives except for the years of World War II when the family was evacuated to concentration camps in the interior of the U.S. Mia and Ryan's parents are Sansei (third generation Japanese American) who met while attending college. Living in Southern California, Mia and Ryan's family have a large, "extended family" of family friends and relations they have known for many many years.

For Your Information
Pronunciation Guide

Japanese words are easy to pronounce if you break them into syllables.
The syllables are unstressed.
Vowels are as follows: **a** as in saw
                        e as in bed
                        i as in ink
                        o as in bone
                        u as in blue

FUYU
WINTER

OSHŌGATSU Morning

"Are we almost there?" Mia asks again from the bench seat of the mini-van.

"Ten more minutes," Dad answers as he exits off the freeway.

The car ride from home to Grandpa and Grandma's house is only about 40 minutes, but five-year-old Mia gets antsy easily, and this morning she is especially tired. Mom rustled her from a deep sleep and made her put on a "nice" dress. "It's New Year's Day," Mom explained.

"Don't forget to say, 'Happy New Year' to Grandma and Grandpa and all the Aunties and Uncles," Mom reminds again as the car pulls into the narrow driveway. "Remember your manners," she calls out as Mia and her brother Ryan trot up the front porch. "At least try and eat a little bit of...everything." her voice fades as the screen door closes.

Grandma and Grandpa's narrow livingroom is a blur of people, shoulder to shoulder on the couch, cross-legged on the carpet, perched on card-table chairs. Uncle Mas, cousins, Brian and Travis, briefly avert their eyes from the football game on TV to greet the most recent arrivals.

"Happy New Year, Happy New Year," Grandma

Oshōgatsu the Japanese New Year holiday. The word, "*Oshōgatsu*" means the "proper season." In Japan, Oshōgatsu is the busiest time of the year. Everyone prepares for the close of the old year and the celebration of the new. To properly end the old year, people try to "tie all loose ends;" settling arguments, completing any business, paying off debts, returning borrowed items, and thoroughly cleaning house. The New Year dawns a clean, fresh beginning.

The Oshōgatsu tradition dates back to the earliest days of Japanese history and its agricultural tradition. Rice is the most important food to the Japanese. The connection to the rice culture is present in many traditions of the Japanese New Year; like the eating of *ozōni* (rice-cake soup), the display of the *okasane* or *kagami-mochi* (decoration of two mochi, topped by a small *dai-dai* or Japanese citrus fruit) the serving of *sake* (rice wine), and display of the *shimenawa* (decoration made of twisted rice straw.).

In the United States the Issei continued the celebration of Oshōgatsu. Many of the traditional foods were not available and young families were far away from extended family and familiar surroundings. Maintaining the Oshōgatsu tradition took on a new and more significant meaning in America. As Prof. Lloyd Inui writes in the publication, **Oshōgatsu (JACCC,**

19

1983):

...the Isseis' conscientious efforts to display the kasane-mochi, organize a mochitsuki, prepare the osechi-ryori, attend a temple or shrine, visit one's friends and relations, and pay one's debts quite possibly take on a new and more significant meaning related directly to the circumstances of the Issei community in America. After all, it was at no small expense of time and money that the osechi-ryōri was prepared and that homes were opened to friends and family with full hospitality, including a plentiful sharing of sake. And given the limited acceptance extended to the Japanese during this time, it was vital for Issei to reaffirm ties with their own countrymen. Oshōgatsu as such may have reflected a pragmatic and functional need. (Oshōgatsu, pg 12,1993).

Omedetō

An abbreviated way to express, "Happy New Year." A more proper way and formal way to say "Happy New Year" is *"Shinnen ake-mashite omedetō gozaimasu."* *"Omedetō"* is a word of congratulations and can be used at almost every happy and celebratory occasion, like weddings, anniversaries, birthdays, etc.

Ōkiku-natta ne

You've grown!. This is a favorite phrase of adults when speaking to children.

Ozōni tabetai

"Do you want to eat ozōni?" Ozōni is the traditional New Year soup featuring

---

calls from the dining room. She is replenishing a large platter of *sushi*. *"Omedetō, mā ōkiku-natta ne,"* Tanaka *Obasan* says as she squeezes Ryan's arm and pats Mia on the head. *"Ozōni tabetai, gud'do, yo.* I make it." she explains and she scurries to the kitchen to put two more *mochi* in the broiler to brown.

Uncle George quickly finishes, Auntie Carol scoots over to make more room at the dining room table. Dirty dishes are cleared and clean plates are brought for the newest arrivals. Two extra leaves have lengthened the dining table to its capacity. The good china is on the table as well as every large platter and bowl. Grandma has brought down from the highest cupboard shelf the *jūbako*, each lacquered tier stacks atop the other forming the picture of a crane in flight. A broiled *tai* and a red lobster compose the table centerpiece. Mia eyes the table cautiously. She recognizes the *inarizushi* and *norimaki*, Grandma's chashu, oooh a big plate of fried shrimp, fried won ton, and chicken salad.

"Nishime? Sunomono? Konbumaki?" Auntie Carol poses her *hashi* over the various dishes. Mia shakes her head. "Come on try a little," Mommy

prods. Mom starts to put a little of everything on her plate. She moves to a bowl of black, round beans. "*Kuromame*, you're supposed to have these. It's for good luck. One for each year of your life." She puts a small spoonful on Mia's plate and a slightly bigger amount on Ryan's.

"Be careful, it's hot," Grandma puts the ozōni in front of the children.

They stab at the sticky rice glob awkwardly with their hashi and pull it apart like white taffy. Mmm, it's good, the children stuff their mouths. As they chew a chatter of voices ring above their heads. "The sushi's good this year, Auntie," "Are Johnny and Wendy and the kids coming?" "What did you guys do for New Year's Eve?" "Boy, Ryan's getting big, isn't he? What grade you in now?" "Eat, eat, there's plenty. More ozōni? Gotta start the New Year off right, y'a know."

mochi
pounded rice cake. Depending on the chef and her/his regional roots in Japan, there are many variations of the soup as far as ingredients and preparation.

Gud'do-yo. I make it.
a combination of Japanese and English in one sentence. "It's good, I made it."

jūbako
tiered, square, lacquered wood (or plastic) box-like containers which stack one on top of the other. Traditionally New Year food or *osechi* is placed in the jūbako.

inarizushi and **norimaki**
the most familiar form of *sushi* or seasoned rice for Japanese Americans. Sushi comes in a variety of forms, served with raw seafood, various prepared vegetables or other ingredients. The "footballs" or inarizushi consist of rice stuffed into small pockets made from prepared soy bean curd. Norimaki is rice vegetables and other ingredients like cooked egg and shrimp rolled in *nori* or seaweed.

nishime
a Japanese dish of stewed vegetables

sunomono
a Japanese side dish of vinegared vegetables

konbu-maki
stewed seaweed packets stuffed with fish

hashi
chopsticks

kuromame
black beans

21

22

ISSEI Generation

The large majority of first generation or Issei Japanese Americans immigrated to the United States over 100 years ago (from the late 1800's to 1924). The Issei came to the United States for the opportunity of a better life. They were adventurous young adults who left their homeland to take on jobs like laborers, farmers and railroad workers with dreams of returning to Japan wealthy and successful men and women.

In the United States, the Issei faced discrimination or unfair treatment because they were of a different race than most of the people living in America. The laws of the United States did not allow Japanese to own their own land, become citizens, or live wherever they chose. The worst and most extreme example of racism against Japanese Americans was the World War II uprooting and evacuation of over 110,000 Japanese Americans (including second-generation Nisei American citizens) from the west coast into concentration camps. The evacuation resulted in loss of property and livelihood, and great personal tragedy and suffering.

The large majority of Issei immigrants did not return to Japan, but raised families and established their own communities — building businesses, churches, temples, language schools, theatres and other institutions in the United States. The Issei laid the foundation of our Japanese American communities and valued their language, religions, and cultural traditions.

Photo: Ed Ikuta

GENERATIONS

Japanese Americans have a unique custom of labeling themselves and each new generation by number, beginning with the Issei or the first generation of Japanese Americans. To count in Japanese from one to ten, say; *ichi, ni, san, shi* (or *yon*), *go, roku, shichi,* (or *nana*), *hachi, ku, jū. Sei* is added to each number and means generation. Issei or first generation is followed by Nisei, Sansei, Yonsei, then *Gosei*. Although the Nisei are the first generation to be born in the United States, they are counted as the second-generation of Japanese Americans. Yonsei Mia and Ryan have Sansei parents and Nisei grandparents. If a person has a Sansei mother and a Nisei father, he/she would be considered a *Sansei-han* or a third-generation plus one-half. This custom of identifying by generation can be difficult or confusing. For example, how do you identify yourself if you are Hapa (one parent is of Japanese heritage and the other is not) or, let's say your Yonsei brother marries a recent post-war immigrant from Japan?

Something to think about. The next time you are in Little Tokyo or Japantown, or at a Japanese American community event, or just listening to members of your family conversing, see if you notice any of these generational words, for example; the Nisei Athletic Union, the Yonsei Basketball Team, or C.D. called "Sansei" by the jazz-fusion band, Hiroshima.

24

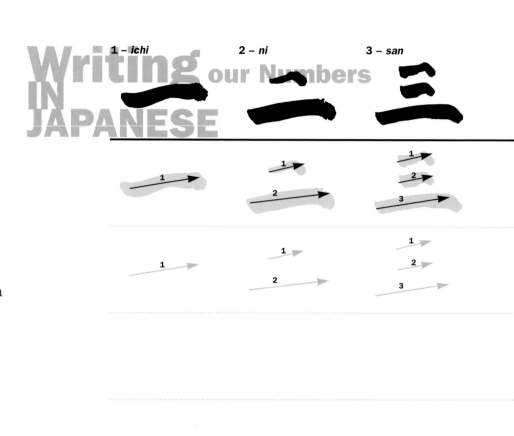

Writing our Numbers IN JAPANESE

1 – *ichi*   2 – *ni*   3 – *san*

4 – shi **5 – go** **6 – roku** **7 – shichi** **8 – hachi** **9 – kyu** **10 – jū**

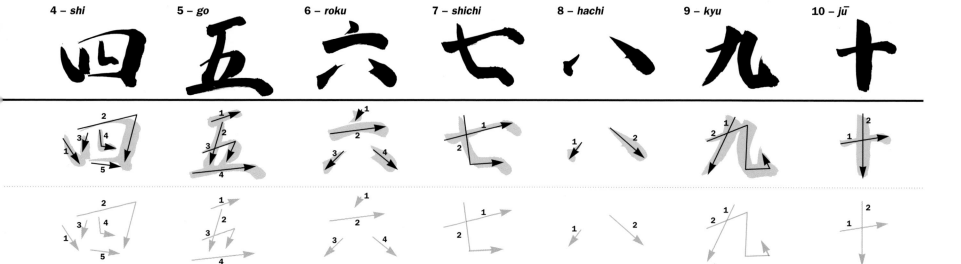

In Winter, BAACHAN would...
By Joyce Nako

Winter, when snow would fall on my life
    blanketing in coldness touched by a fever;
So cold my bones would ache and I'd shiver
    under deep deep piles of blankets,
        I remember Baachan handing to me
        soda crackers and Seven-Up

        Okayu in a bowl
        A round ball of red
        Surrounded by white:
        Umeboshi to spike
        the meal

The Umeboshi crinkled my face,
it was
So very salty
But I liked to have a little bite of it
A spoonful of the sticky wet gruel;
A balance my mouth liked
very much

        In Winter
While cold and wet and lonely
Baachan fed me love and tenderness
That's why I love being sick today.

In sunshine
I'd hold my Baachan's hand
We walked fast
To the store
I'd run to keep up
And she only walked fast

She could exercise
With her whole hands
Touching the ground
When she bent over
Back straight
All the way down
        I can't do that
        My back is tight

Her hair is white
Shiroi like snow
Her face is wrinkled
Her smile is widest
when she looks at me
        So I like it when she looks at me

Her body is dumpy
and round
and nice

She wears only dresses
patterned with tiny flowers
Browns and greys, but mostly brown

Her hair is white, like driven snow
My hair is black
But I want white hair
Like hers

In Winter
I remember Baachan would...

Itadakimasu and GOCHISŌSAMA

In Japanese and in many Japanese American homes, it is customary to say, "*Itadakimasu*" before beginning a meal, and "*Gochisōsama*" after finishing eating.

Itadakimasu literally means "to place on one's head." In Japan when receiving an object or gift, traditionally one raises the object to one's head and bows slightly. This is a gesture of gratitude and appreciation. When we say, "Itadakimasu" we are acknowledging respectfully all the people, causes, and conditions involved in preparing the meal. "Gochisōsama" is an expression we say after eating a meal. *Chisō-sama* is the person who "runs busily back and forth," referring to the person who expends energy to prepare the meal. To say, "Gochisōsama" acknowledges the effort of others who made our meal possible.

28

Photo: Bill Ross

OSECHI Ryōri: The New Year FEAST

Osechi **is the traditional Japanese New Year meal.** At one time these dishes were likely considered simple and common, but today many of the ingredients have become rare, and in some cases, like *kazu-no-ko* (fish roe) a luxury. Many of the dishes are prepared in advance and selected because they keep well. For after the hard work of preparing for the New Year, the woman of the family usually took a break from daily cooking the first three days of the New Year.

The Issei generation continued the tradition of preparing the osechi meal in the U.S. Despite the considerable expense, it was important to preserve the tradition in a new country and maintain ties with neighbors and friends.

Nisei and Sansei families have continued the tradition of the New Year osechi today. In many instances, preparing the meal is a collaborative affair, a Japanese American "potluck" where family members and friends will volunteer or are assigned particular dishes. Many aspects of the meal have been maintained while new dishes more popular with the younger people are added.

There are several foods and dishes considered essentials of the osechi and many of these have "symbolic" meaning and significance, for example, *ozōni,* a mochi or rice-cake soup. The ingredients and preparation for ozōni may vary in different geographic regions of Japan, but the pounded sticky rice cake is always present. We eat ozōni for good luck and prosperity in the coming New Year.

tai, sea bream, a fish roasted whole, positioned so that the body arches like a half-circle. Serving the tai is "good-luck" because its name is contained in the word *omedetai,* which means congratulatory.

kuromame, black soy beans. *Mame* is the word for beans and can also mean good health. For good health, it is customary to eat at least one bean for each year of one's life.

kazu-no-ko, prepared herring roe. This is another play on words, for kazu-no-ko can also mean "lots of children," signifying a wish for many healthy children.

konbu-maki, rolled kelp. *Konbu* sounds like the last syllable of *yorokobu* and means to be glad or joyful.

kuri kinton, sweet potato or lima bean paste with chestnuts. Kuri means to repeat and kin means gold, meaning prosperity and wealth.

Kanto-style
refers to a region in Japan in the eastern part of central Honshu (the main island, which includes the city of Tokyo.

satoimo
potato-like vegetable

mizuna
Japanese leafy green, like a mustard green

shiitake
Japanese mushroom

kamaboko
fishcake

konbu
a type of dried seaweed

Hondashi
a packaged Japanese soupstock

DAISY NAKAI'S OZŌNI Recipe
(Kanto Style)

Ingredients

4 small *shiitake* (cut in half)

4 small *satoimo*

1/2 bunch *mizuna*

1 chicken breast (cut into 8 pieces)

2 tsp *Hondashi*

1 tsp salt

1 tsp shōyu or soy sauce

Konbu

4 small mochi

4 slices of red *kamaboko*

Begin with the *dashi* (or soupstock)

Wash shiitake, remove stems and soak in water for 15 minutes. (Don't throw away the water.)

Scrub satoimo and boil with skin until tender. Remove skin after the satoimo is boiled.

Wash mizuna and boil for 1 minute. Drain and cut into 2-inch pieces.

Boil chicken in 3 cups of water and 1 cup of water that you saved from shiitake. Add 2 tsp. Hondashi, 1 tsp. salt and 1 tsp. shōyu to the broth and bring to a boil.

To cook *mochi*:

Cut a piece of konbu to fit bottom of small pan, then add 2 C of water and bring to a boil. Add mochi and cook for about 1 minute. Be careful not to melt the mochi.

To arrange:

Place mochi on the bottom of the bowl. Add chicken, satoimo, shiitake, and kamaboko. Place mizuna on top. Pour soup on top of everything.

Coloring Winter FOODS

These are some Japanese foods associated with winter. Do you recognize them? Have you eaten them before?

gobō

renkon

mizuna

kuri

mikan

daikon

31

Eating JAPANESE FOOD

In comparing a Western meal and a Japanese meal, there are many differences. A Western meal has a main course served on a single large plate. It is preceded by hors d'oeuvres or a salad and ends with a dessert. A traditional Japanese meal has no main course, but is made up of many small dishes of different types of food, each served on its own plate.

When preparing a Japanese meal, the visual quality or the appearance of the food is very important. Menus are planned around the changing seasons, using the fruits, vegetables and other foods of the current season. Meals are served in small portions, neatly arranged in small plates and bowls, carefully selected for their variety, shape, color, and appropriateness to the season. For example, in the summertime when the weather is hot, a dish of cold noodles will be served in a glass dish to communicate a refreshing coolness. In the wintertime, *nabe-mono* or a meal cooked at the table in an earthenware pot of seafood or meat and vegetables is served.

OBĀCHAN'S Rules

Just like you don't chew with your mouth full, or slurp your soup, or put your elbows on the table when you eat American food, there are rules to follow when eating Japanese style.

When eating with *waribashi* or disposable wooden chopsticks, don't scrape the sticks against each other to take off small slivers of wood.

You can slurp when drinking Japanese soup or noodles.

When you eat with *hashi* or chopsticks, don't point with them or wave them around in the air while you're eating.

Never leave your hashi sticking upright in the *gohan* or rice. In between bites, return your hashi to the side of your plate or on your *hashi-oki* or chopstick rests.

Don't pierce your food with your hashi, but hold your food between the two sticks.

Never pass food to another person from your hashi to their hashi.

When eating gohan,(let's say you are right-hand-ed) pick up the *chawan* or ricebowl and rest it on your left hand, palm up, fingers together with your thumb gripping the side of the chawan.Using your hashi take the rice with your right hand.

When selecting your food from a larger serving dish, either use separate serving hashi or reverse your own. Put food from the serving dish into your own bowl, and then eat directly from your own bowl. (Don't put food directly to your mouth from the serving dish.)

When drinking soup, it's o.k. to pick up the *owan* or soup bowl. Use hashi to eat the solid ingredients and raise the bowl to your lips to drink the soup. Remember making a slurping sound is o.k. In fact, it makes it easier to drink if the soup is very hot.

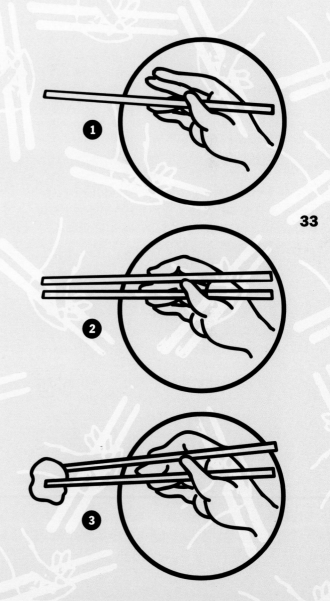

How to **Eat** with **HASHI**

MOCHItsuki

A mochitsuki is the making of *mochi* or rice-cakes. The sticky, dense mounds of rice are made from *mochigome,* a sweeter stickier type of rice, different from the steamed rice eaten every day. *Mochitsuki* is a New Year tradition because eating mochi is an important part of the celebration. In the old days, both in Japan and in the Japanese American community, mochi was pounded by hand, using wooden mallets called a *kine* against an *usu* or large stone or wooden mortar. Temples, churches, and extended families would pound the New Year mochi in an all-day event which included lots of socializing, eating and drinking. Today most of the mochi is produced by machine and purchased at local Japanese confectionery and grocery stores. The tradition of pounding mochi, however, is still continued by some temples, churches, community organizations, and families.

34

MOCHI, Mochi, MOCHI

Mochi remains an ever-popular treat for Japanese Americans. When asked the question, "How do you eat your mochi?" the responses were:

Toasted in the broiler and wrapped in *nori (*seaweed) with a little shōyu.

Toasted in the broiler and dipped in *sato-shōyu,* (a mixture of sugar and soy sauce).

Freshly made, dipped in *kinako (*roasted then sweetened soy-bean powder) or toasted with shōyu and sugar.

I invented eating mochi with kinako and honey.

Roasted on an open fire until it's *kitsune-iro* (golden brown), with a little shōyu.

When freshly made, torn into bite-sized pieces, dropped in *natto* (fermented soybeans) with shōyu and *wasabi* (Japanese mustard).

When it's fresh, I eat it plain, just like it is, and I chew it very slowly.

I like small pieces of fresh mochi with grated *toro-ro-imo* (Japanese wild yam root), dashi (soup stock), shōyu, and, *aonori* (a kind of seaweed) sprinkled on the top. I think eating mochi like this comes from a northern Japanese tradition.

To me, mochi goes with anything, when I'm hungry and want a little something more, I put it in Lipton's Chicken Noodle soup or minestrone.

I like it in my noodles, it's called *chikara udon*.

Sometimes I crave *oshiruko,* mochi in a sweet bean soup.

After my family has had its fill of ozōni, we always deep-fry thin slices of mochi.

At the Vista Obon carnival every summer they sell a delicious fried mochi dipped in *goma* or sesame seeds.

I dip my mochi into shōyu and freshly grated *shoga* (ginger)

With *daikon oroshii* (or freshly grated Japanese radish) and shōyu.

At our family mochitsuki, we make some batches of mochi with raisins added. When it's toasted, it reminds me of a bagel.

Zap frozen mochi in the microwave for 30-40 seconds, and then cook in a non-stick pan and eat with nori and a little shōyu.

When I cook *sukiyaki* (main dish of meat and vegetables), I like to put mochi in the pan at the very end of the meal. It soaks up all those tasty juices and tastes really good.

When I was a kid I ate my mochi with peanut butter and jam.

First I toast the mochi in the toaster oven, then I put it in a chawan and sprinkle salt on top, and then pour hot tea over it.

Photo: Ed Ikuta

"Be My NEW YEAR GOOD-LUCK Charms"

There are many good-luck symbols that are associated with the New Year and other important or happy occasions, like the *tsuru*, or Japanese crane, and the *kame*, or turtle. Both are popular Japanese symbols of long life and happiness. As motifs they appear on paintings, prints, fabric designs, ceramics and other works of art and crafts.

Because the tsuru symbolize health and long life, it is a Japanese tradition to fold 1,000 paper cranes or *senbazuru* for someone who is seriously ill. One of the most famous stories associated with the folding of 1,000 cranes is the story of the little girl, Sadako, who was a victim of the atomic bombing of Hiroshima during World War II. Stricken with leukemia, Sadako attempted to fold the 1,000 cranes with the hope of regaining her health. She was not able to complete the task before her death in 1955, but her story became a symbol throughout the nation of the human

tragedy that resulted from the atomic bomb and the need to work towards world peace. In Peace Park in the city of Hiroshima, a monument was built to honor the memory of those who died from the atomic bomb. Atop the monument is a statue of Sadako, holding in her hands a folded crane. Children from Japan and all over the world send 1,000 cranes to Hiroshima to be displayed on the monument. Whenever you visit Peace Park, the paper cranes are draped around Sadako as a reminder of the need for world peace.

Origami TSURU

Beginning with a square piece of paper...

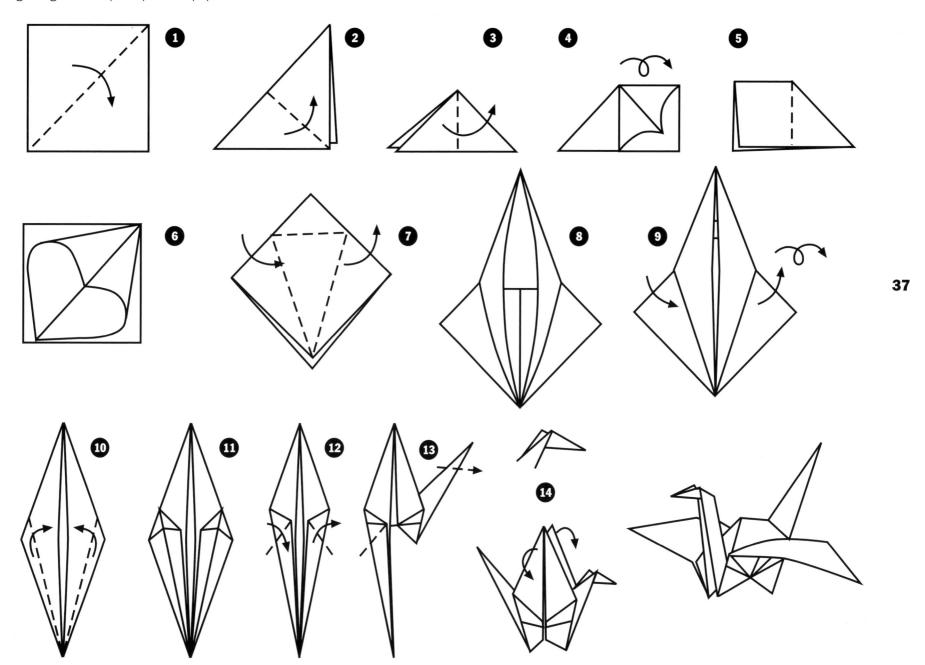

Origami KAME

Beginning with a square piece of paper...

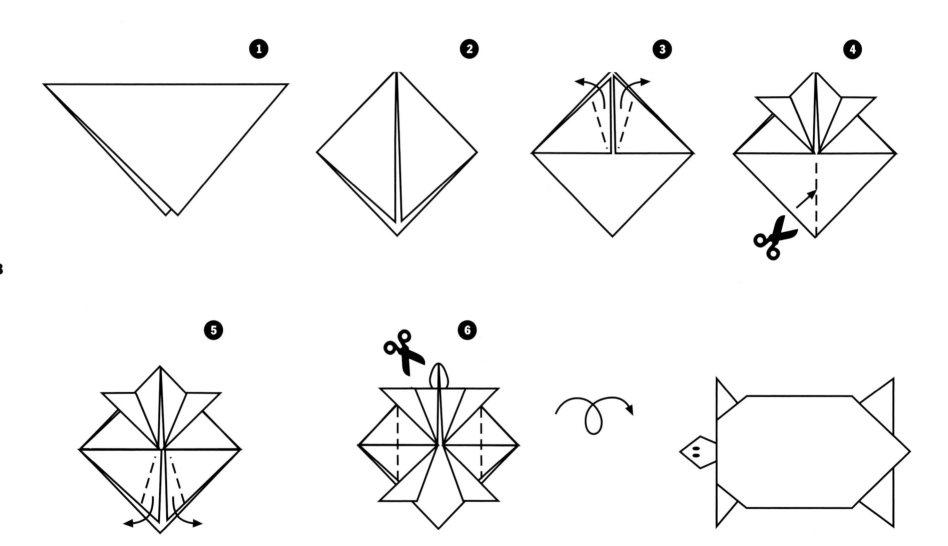

Daruma

Another popular New Year charm is the *daruma*. This distinctive wood or papier-mache, round-bottomed doll with its rather fierce-looking face is sold at outdoor fairs in Japan as a good luck charm. The daruma is modeled after a Buddhist monk, Bodhidharma who sat in meditation for so many years that he lost use of his arms and legs. Despite these disabilities, Bodhidharma continued his practicing and teaching of Zen Buddhism. The daruma is a symbol of perseverance; never giving up and always trying one's best.

Daruma Coloring Page
Color the Daruma, but only draw in one eye. Write your wish at the bottom of the page. When your wish comes true, draw in the other eye.

ANIMAL Zodiac

A full cycle of the Chinese zodiac is 12 years, with each year represented by a different animal. People born in a particular animal year are believed to hold personality traits associated with that animal. The animal representing the current new year will be a popular symbol for New Year festivities, appearing on cards, calendars, and decorations.

According to Japanese custom, there are also certain birthdays which are especially important, critical or auspicious, such as the 33rd, 42nd, 60th and 88th. In celebration of these birthdays, the Animal year of the celebrant will also be a prominent feature in the festivities.

Japanese memorize the order of the animals by the following abbreviations: *ne, ushi, tora, u, tatsu, mi, uma, hitsuji, saru, tori, inu,i.* The animals of the zodiac in proper order are:

40

Rat (*nezumi*)
1924, 1936, 1948, 1960, 1972, 1984, 1996, 2008, 2020
Charming and also fussy about small matters; when they want something they are willing to work very hard to attain their goals. Honest and ambitious, those born in the Year of the Rat are thrifty and like to spend money on themselves.

Ox (*ushi*)
1925, 1937, 1949, 1961, 1973, 1985, 1997, 2009, 2021
Reticent and patient, a person born in the Year of the Ox can also be very stubborn and rash. Slightly eccentric, they are mentally very alert.

Horse (*uma*)
1918, 1930, 1942, 1954, 1966, 1978, 1990, 2002, 2014
Hot-blooded and talented, people born in the Year of the Horse are quick in everything they do. They are also flashy in their dress and manner and popular with others.

Sheep (*hitsuji*)
1919, 1931, 1943, 1955, 1967, 1979, 1991, 2003, 2015
People born in the Year of the Sheep are shy, pessimistic and often puzzled over life. They are wise, gentle, elegant, and highly accomplished in the arts.

Tiger (*tora*)
1926, 1938, 1950, 1962, 1974, 1986, 1998, 2010, 2022
Courageous and stubborn, the Tiger is one of the strongest signs of the zodiac. Suspicious and short-tempered, they are also sensitive and deep-thinking.

Rabbit (*usagi*)
1927, 1939, 1951, 1963, 1975, 1987, 1999, 2011, 2023
Talented, virtuous, and financially lucky, people born in the Year of the Rabbit are the most fortunate. They are affectionate and by nature placid and do not easily lose their tempers.

Dragon (*tatsu*)
1928, 1940, 1952, 1964, 1976, 1988, 2000, 2012, 2024
Excitable, brave and honest, people born in the Year of the Dragon are also short-tempered and stubborn. They can accomplish good work and can inspire trust in others.

Snake (*hebi*)
1929, 1941, 1953, 1965, 1977, 1989, 2001, 2013, 2025
Intense, though calm by nature, people born in the Year of the Snake are determined in whatever they do. They can be vain and selfish, but also possess tremendous wisdom.

Monkey (*saru*)
1920, 1932, 1944, 1956, 1968, 1980, 1992, 2004, 2016
Inventive and original, Year of the Monkey people are good problem-solvers. Passionate and strong natured, they tend to cool off quickly.

Rooster (*tori*)
1921, 1933, 1945, 1957, 1969, 1981, 1993, 2005, 2017
People born in the Year of the Rooster always think they are right. Deep-thinkers, busy and devoted to their work, sometimes they take on more than they are able to handle.

Dog (*inu*)
1922, 1934, 1946, 1958, 1970, 1982, 1994, 2006, 2018
Honest, loyal and possessing a deep sense of duty, people born in the Year of the Dog always do their best in relationships with others. However, they are not good at social gatherings and can be very critical.

Boar (*inoshishi*)
1923, 1935, 1947, 1959, 1971, 1983, 1995, 2007, 2019
Possessing an inner strength, people born in the Year of the Boar cannot be deterred from a goal. They are well-informed and study a great deal. Boars don't make many friends, but keep their friends for life.

42

HARU
SPRING

43

HINAMATSURI Girl's Day

Sandy, Mia's mom, took a large cardboard box down from the locked cupboard in the attic and carried it to the living room floor. Curious, Mia hovered around her mother.

"What are you doing, Mommy? Can I help? What's this? Can I open it?"

"You can help, Mia, but sit down first and don't grab. These things are very old and very fragile."

As her mother began to take the small *furoshiki* wrapped bundles and smaller cardboard boxes from the carton, Mia recognized the contents from the year before. These were her Japanese dolls, the dolls for *Hinamatsuri* or Girl's Day. Sandy began to line up the miniatures of Japanese royalty, carefully wrapped in layers and layers of tissue paper.

"The ladies in waiting, the musicians...what's this? A lantern... here's a branch of peach blossoms."

Mia burrowed into the bottom of the big box, she was looking for the *odairisama*, the royal couple. They were nestled in a cedar box and Mia unwrapped them carefully like a true treasure. The

Hinamatsuri
the Doll Festival is a celebration for Japanese girls and is held each year on March 3. According to custom, when a girl is born in a Japanese family, she receives a set of dolls which represent the court of Heian Japan (794-1185). The dolls are displayed on Girl's Day and a special meal is prepared.

furoshiki
a square piece of cloth used to wrap and carry things. Furoshiki literally means bath spread and its usage originates from when a bather at a bath house was given a piece of cloth to put his clothes in so that they would not get wet.

Furoshiki come in all sizes and are made from a variety of fabrics.

odairisama
the royal couple of the Heian Court. Traditionally, Hinamatsuri dolls are displayed with respect and reverence as they portray Japanese royalty, one-time considered descendants of the gods. Special meals and foods are offered to the dolls as part of the ritual celebration. Traditionally *amazake*, a sweet drink made of rice with hishimochi, a tricol-

45

ored red, white, and green rice cake are served to guests.

kimono
traditional Japanese clothing. For an occasion like Girl's Day, a young girl would wear a formal kimono made of silk.

kokeshi
originally a folk toy. Kokeshi are simple dolls crafted from wood with cylindrical bodies, no arms or legs and a spherical head.

headpiece of the Empress had slipped from her head and caught into her long black hair. Mia secured the doll's head piece, tidied her hair and then searched for the little fan that is to be placed in her tiny hands. Mia thought the Emperor's long narrow hat funny and told her mother it looked like he was wearing a tail on his head.

The dolls originally belonged to her Mommy's Auntie Eiko. Auntie Eiko was a *kibei*, born in the U.S. but as a child sent to Japan to be educated. She returned to the U.S. to rejoin her family just before the outbreak of World War II. From Japan, Eiko brought with her the set of traditional Japanese dolls and many other beautiful things. Because she had no daughters, she gave her dolls to Mia's mother, Sandy.

Over the years, some of the accessories, like the musical instruments and the kitchen utensils have broken or become lost, so the set was not quite complete. Sandy usually set up tiered shelves on a red cloth covering the small end table in the corner of the family room. She encouraged Mia to include her collection of *kokeshi* dolls and all her Barbies alongside the Japanese dolls. It was quite an impressive display.

Last year when she was four years old, Mia was dressed in a beautiful *kimono* that had belonged to her mother when she was a little girl. Daddy took her picture standing next to her dolls and made copies for all the grandparents and aunts and uncles. Grandma and Grandpa brought over the pink and white rice cracker treat, *hina-arare*, just for Girl's Day and the *sakura-mochi* or Japanese sweet.

Something to THINK ABOUT

The traditional hina-matsuri dolls are very costly and not affordable for most families with young children. Even in Japan there are variations on the observance. You can purchase just the odairisama or make an origami display. A family project might be a fabric wall-hanging with applique dolls. Maybe there are Japanese antique shops in your neighborhood: sometimes you can find dolls in wonderful condition. Be creative and you can come up with a pretty and personal hinamatsuri display.

Origami **HINA DOLL**

Beginning with a square piece of paper...

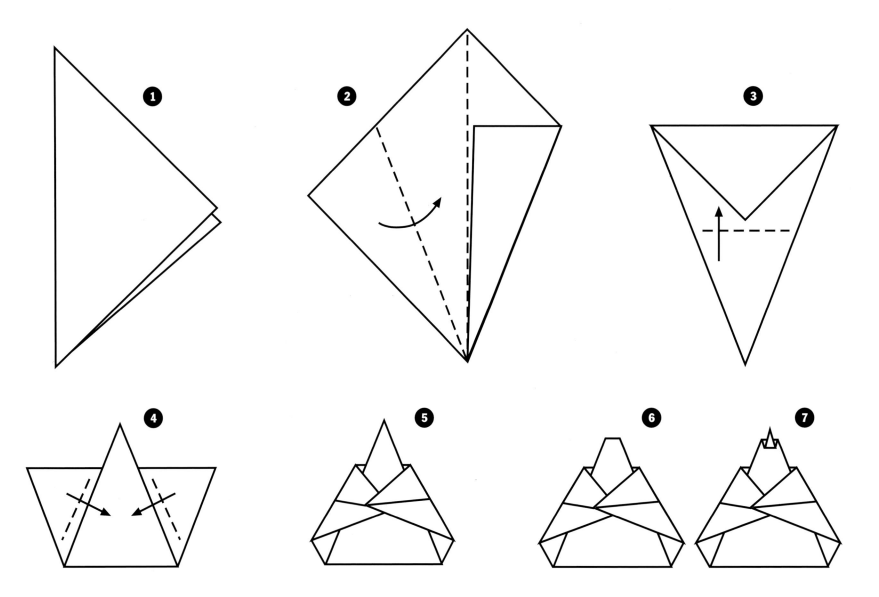

KIMONO
Traditional JAPANESE Clothes

Kimono are traditional Japanese clothes. Made of vertical panels of cloth stitched together, the kimono is bound with a sash or *obi*. During the Heian period (794-1185) members of the court wore as many as twelve layers of thin, flowing, silk kimono. Harmonizing the colors of the overlapping layers according to the season and an aesthetic sense was an artistic challenge for the wearer. By the 14th century, the kimono was simplified to a more simple garment secured with the obi.

Today there remain rules and considerations when wearing a kimono, depending on the wearer's age, the season and the occasion. The choice of colors, designs, and materials cannot be done casually. For the most informal occasions and the hot summer months a *yukata* or unlined cotton kimono is worn. For special events, like weddings and funerals a *montsuki* or black silk kimono marked with the family crest is worn. Young girls wear *furisode* or brightly colored kimono with long flowing sleeves, while married women wear more subtle colors, with subdued patterns and shorter sleeves.

Men and boys wear kimono of simpler, often geometric patterns, shorter sleeves and earthtone colors.

49

Photo: Ed Ikuta

Designing a KIMONO

Try designing your own kimono. You can use a simple, overall pattern, like a fan or arrow. Or use images from nature, like flowers, birds, and butterflies. Stripes and geometric shapes are also popular, especially for boys and men. Is your kimono for a young girl? A married lady? What colors are best for your design and the person you have in mind?

50

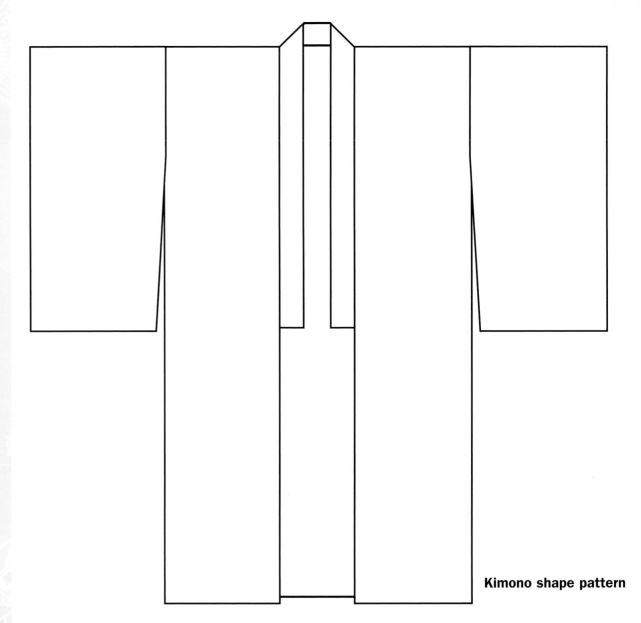

Kimono shape pattern

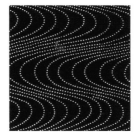

PROPER B O W

Whether dressed in kimono or Western clothes, the traditional Japanese greeting is expressed with a bow or *ojigi*. Here in the United States people greet each other with a handshake, but there are still times when we will be greeted with a bow and expected to bow in return. Maybe you will study Japanese dance or a martial art, like karate or aikidō. A proper bow is an important part of study and shows respect to your teacher and for your art form.

There are different kinds of bows, depending on how formal or informal the occasion. Hints for a proper ordinary bow made while standing up are: Stand upright and look forward.

Women place their hands together to form an inverted "v" and rest them on their thighs.

Men place their hands apart on each thigh or keep them at their side.

Bend the body to an angle, while sliding your hands to your knees. After a short pause, lift your head and straighten your body.

Do not bend at a sharp angle at the hips.

Do not lower just your head.

Do not "bob your head" and move in a jerky fashion.

Photos: Ed Ikuta

Sakura

Sakura or cherry blossoms is the national flower of Japan and a popular symbol of spring. In early April the cherry blossoms are usually in full bloom and a favorite attraction for people all over Japan. Since the 8th century, a favorite custom is cherry blossom-viewing parties where picnics are planned under the beautiful blossoming cherry trees.

The cherry blossom was also an important symbol to *samurai* or Japanese warriors, who identified with the delicate blossoms that bloomed briefly, then were scattered away by a spring breeze. A brief, but brilliant life, reflected the spirit of the samurai who were expected to fight bravely in the face of sudden death. The fragile sakura remind us all that life is precious and fleeting.

An outing to view the flowers is called a *hanami*. Japanese Americans have continued this tradition of hanami here in the U.S. While there are not blossoming cherry trees, Issei, Nisei and Sansei plan trips to view colorful wild flowers and other desert flowers. Car caravans or busloads of young and old drive out to places like Lancaster, California to picnic, walk amid the poppies and enjoy one another's company.

52

Make a **SAKURA** Decoration

Materials:

tissue paper (dark pink and light pink)

tissue paper (dark green and light green)

small white straws

several large beads

white thread

needle

waribashi or wooden chopsticks

Instructions:

Cut out the flower and leaf shapes.

Using the flower shape as a guide, trace many more flower shapes onto the dark and light pink tissue paper. Cut these flower shapes out.

Using the leaf shape as a guide, trace many more leaf shapes onto the dark and light green tissue paper. Cut these leaf shapes out.

Cut the straws into 1/2-inch lengths.

Tie a bead onto the end of a piece of thread. Using the needle, string the shapes, alternating the flower shapes, the leaf shapes and straw pieces. It doesn't matter how you string the pieces just do whatever you think is pretty.

Depending on how large you want your sakura decoration to be, vary the length of the thread. When you finish, you can tie your strand to the end of a waribashi or long thin stick. Or, you can tie many shorter, single strands to a long stick and extend it across the doorway of your room.

Adapted from Carolyn K. Morinishi, "Kodomo Korner," *KaMai Forum*. April 1995

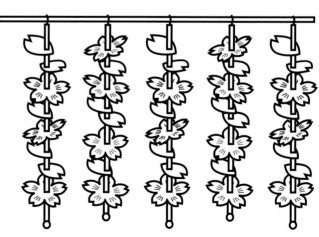

THE Importance of Being CHANTO

By **Naomi Hirahara**

When referring to the philosophies of the Issei in the U.S., Japanese Americans use such terms as *gaman* (perseverance) and *enryo* (reserve).

I'd like to offer another one — *chanto.*

Chanto is one of these Japanese colloquialisms that doesn't have exact English equivalent. Literally, it means "in good order," "thoroughly," and "properly," but in practice, it covers much more.

Anybody raised by a Japanese-influenced parent or grandparent has heard the phrase "chanto shinasai," or "be chanto." It can be said in reference to an upturned shirt collar, talking too loud, mowing the lawn, shoving dollar bills into an already overstuffed pocket, arriving to an appointment late, chewing gum at a funeral, or paying bills late.

I, myself, am a chanto rebel. My natural inclination is toward the intangibles — feelings, principles, spirituality — and not the tangible. Rules, they're meant to be broken. Ask me my thoughts about any controversy and I'll comply, but ask me about where I left my coffee cup that morning, and I'll probably be stumped.

It's nothing to do with my upbringing — my *shin* Issei mother is the master of chanto. But ever since childhood, I was always losing my sweater or laughing too loud. Definitely a chanto mother's nightmare.

But the older I get and the more I observe the Japanese American community, I see the value of chanto. A yes means yes, and no means no. If you say you will do it, you will do it. It's very simple, but so rare in this fast-paced society of empty promises:

"Let's get together sometime."

"I'll have it ready by the end of the day."

"I'll take care of it."

"The check is in the mail."

We've all said and heard these things, but have we always followed through? Have we thought, "Well, it really doesn't matter, tomorrow is a new today."

When we plan some sort of event, do we settle for the haphazard, do we just think everything will somehow miraculously come together without having our bases covered? Do we cut corners? Do we commit ourselves to a project or group without having any intention to hold up our responsibility?

Admittedly, today's society is so high-pressured; we can literally drive ourselves crazy about being anal retentive and detail oriented. And to demonstrate ritual without heart is worthless.

But there is something to be said about being chanto in this day and age. With the Issei and Nisei populations fading away, this is one principle that needs to go on.

From the "Ochazuke" Column.

Reprinted with permission from the *Rafu Shimpo*.

TANGO NO SEKKU and K O D O M O N O H I
Boy's Day
Children's Day

Japanese boys have their own holiday, known as *Tango no Sekku* celebrated on May 5. The origins of the festival date back to ancient times, but its more familiar aspects date back to the Tokugawa period with its display of warrior dolls, battle arms, and banners.

A popular symbol of the celebration is the flying of *koinobori* or colorful carp banners. Households with sons will fly a cloth or paper carp from tall poles, one for each son in the family. The *koi* represent valued male traits like courage, strength and perseverance, for the fish is known to swim boldly upstream in its efforts to spawn.

Other activities associated with Boy's Day are kite flying and the eating of traditional foods like: *kashiwamochi*, a sweet mochi filled with sweet bean paste and wrapped in oak leaves; and *chimaki*, another sweet mochi wrapped in bamboo leaves.

On 1948 Tango no Sekku was officially changed to *Kodomo-no-hi* or Children's Day by the Occupational Government under U.S. General Douglas McArthur. This was part of the effort to de-emphasize feudalistic attitudes.

The early Issei immigrants settling in the U.S. continued the tradition of flying koinobori on Boy's Day, and today Nisei grandparents still acknowledge the birth of sons and grandsons with gifts of warrior dolls and samurai helmets or *kabuto*. In the United States, Japanese American communities celebrate their own version of Children's Day. In Little Tokyo, Los Angeles, the first week-end in May activities include a just-for-kids mini-run, the Chibi-K, exhibits of traditional crafts, cultural activities for kids, performances, games, and food booths.

57

Making a
KOINOBORI

Materials:

crayons or markers

scissors

a waribashi or wooden chopstick

length of string, approximately 18 inches

hole punch

Procedure:

Color the koi with crayons or markers.

Cut out your koi by following the outline and cutting out the center section.

Fold the koi in half length-wise

Using the hole punch, punch a hole at the koi's mouth.

Attach one end of the string to your waribashi and tie the other to the koi

58

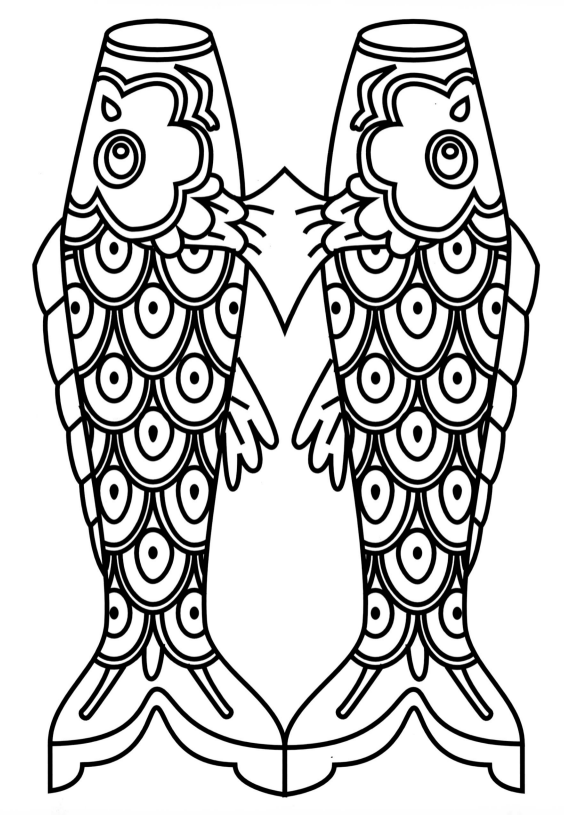

Gyotaku is a print made of a real fish.

Gyo means fish in Japanese and *taku* means stone monument rubbing. Long ago fisherman would make a print of fish to record their size and the type of fish caught. Artists saw the beauty of this method of print-making and began to make them for exhibit and as decorations on fans, scrolls, and even on articles of clothing.

Materials

A whole fish. (Uncleaned so that is still has its scales.) Look for a fish with well defined, thick scales.)

Cookie sheet or tray

Paint brush (soft bristles)

Water-based printing ink, red or black

Paper (rice paper works well, newsprint, paper towels and tissue paper will work, too.)

Procedure:

Rinse the fish with water and dry thoroughly.

Place the fish on the cookie sheet and try to spread out its fin and tail so it lies flat.

Pour some ink into a paper cup and stir so that it is a nice creamy consistency. If it is too thick, dilute it with a little water.

Brush an even coat of ink all over the fish. Then lay a piece of paper over the fish and pat gently. Don't forget the tail and the fins.

Gently lift off the paper and you have a finished print.

If you like, you can mount your finished print on a piece of construction paper.

Nihon
Japan

ojīsan
old man

obāsan
old woman

momo
peach

don bura koko
sound of a peach floating

60 **ogyā, ogyā**
sound of a baby crying

oni
demons

oishii
delicious

otōsan
father

okāsan
mother

kibidango
dumpling made of rice

inu
dog

wan, wan, wan
sound of dog barking

kiji
pheasant

ken, ken, ken
sound of a bird

saru
monkey

kya, kya, kya
sound of monkey

itai
ouch! oww! It hurts.

Gomen nasai!
Forgive me!

The Story of MOMOTARŌ
Adapted by **Michiko Tagawa**

A Short Play with Stick Puppets.

(See puppet characters at the end of the play.)

CAST OF CHARACTERS:
Baby Momotarō
Momotarō the Peach Boy
Ojīsan the Old Man
Obāsan the Old Woman
Inu the Dog
Kiji the Pheasant
Saru the Monkey
Narrator
Oni Chief the Demon Chief
Oni Demons

Narrator Long, long ago in the land of Nihon, there lived an Ojīsan and Obāsan.

One day the Ojīsan went to the woods to gather firewood and his wife went to the river to do the washing. The Obāsan was surprised to see a huge peach floating down the river. (The sound of a peach floating) *Don bura kokko... don bura kokko.*

Obāsan picked up the giant peach and took it home.

(Enter Ojīsan) Soon the Ojīsan came home. He was hungry.

Ojīsan I'm hungry. Is dinner ready?

Narrator Obāsan showed him the huge peach and just as she was going to cut it open, it burst open by itself and out jumped a little boy.

Momotarō Ogyā, ogyā, ogyā!

Narrator Because he was born from a peach, the Ojīsan and Obāsan named him Momotarō, which means "Peach Boy."

Momotarō soon grew up into a very strong, gentle and intelligent lad.

At that time, there lived many Oni or demons on the Isle of Oni. They often raided the towns and villages, frightening all the townspeople.

Oni Wha, wha, wha

Oni Chief Oni, do you like to eat people?

Oni Ya, ya, ya

Oni #1 Oishii, people are so delicious.

Demons Ya, ya, ya

Oni #2 I like to eat cheeks.

Oni Ya, ya, ya

Oni #3: I like legs. Mmmm, they're good.

Narrator One day Momotarō went to his mother and father.

Momotarō Otōsan, Okāsan. I must go and punish those Oni on the Isle of the Oni.

Narrator The Ojīsan gave him a sword and the Obāsan made him a good lunch of *kibidango*. On the way, Momotarō met an Inu.

Inu Wan, wan, wan.

Narrator A Kiji

Kiji Ken, ken, ken

Narrator And a Saru

Saru Kya, kya, kya

Narrator Momotarō shared the kibidango with each of them and they became good friends.

Inu, Kiji & Saru Here comes Mo- Mo-Ta-Rō now!

Narrator They got on a boat and sailed across the sea to the Isle of the Oni.

Momotarō Open up the Gate!

Oni What are you doing here?

Momotarō We came to clobber you and punish you!

Narrator With that Momotarō and his friends kicked open the gate. The Inu bit at the Oni. The Saru scratched at the Oni, and the Kiji pecked at the Oni.

Oni Itai! Itai!

Oni Chief Itai! Itai! Have mercy on me. Please don't kill me.

Narrator The Oni apologized and returned the treasures they had stolen from the people.

Oni Gomen nasai. We promise never to do wrong again!

Narrator So Momotarō and his friends, the Inu, Kiji and Saru forgave the Oni and returned home to the Ojīsan and Obāsan in good spirits. And ever since then, there has been peace in the villages and towns.

All Mo-Mo-Ta-Rō! Mo-Mo-Ta-Rō!

62

Make your own Stick PUPPETS

Materials:

tongue depressors or popsicle sticks

construction paper

scissors

glue

Procedure:

Photocopy and enlarge characters.

Color each of the characters.

Cut out the characters for the play and mount them on sturdier paper with glue.

Glue your sticks onto the back of each character.

Let the story begin.

Baby Momotaro

Narrator

Momotaro

Ojīsan

Obāsan

Inu

Kiji

Saru

Oni Chief

Oni

Oni

Oni

Making a KABUTO
(Warriors Helmet)
TO WEAR

Materials:

1 large square
sheet of paper,
about 21 x21"

markers or poster
paints

1 large round stick-
er, about, 3"

Procedure:

Follow drawings to
fold kabuto.

You can secure the
front with a sticker
or seal.

Paint or decorate
with markers.

64

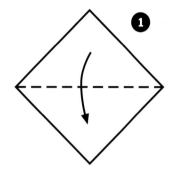
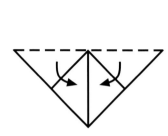
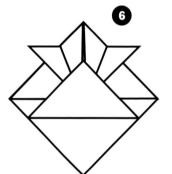
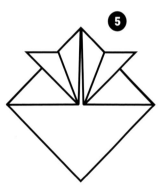

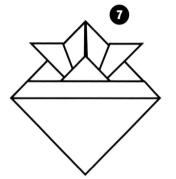
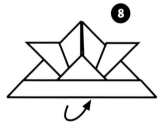

JAN, KEN, PON...

Jan Ken Pon is a popular hand-game and a quick way to decide the winner or the loser, like flipping a coin, "heads or tails." Begin the game by holding one hand up in a fist next to your shoulder; bring it down in front of you as you call out "*jan.*" Repeat this action, but call out **"*ken,*"** the second time your hand comes down. The third time, as you call out "*pon,*" show one of three hand symbols; for rock, scissors or paper. All the players do this at the same time, so no one knows which symbol the other will show.

The winner is determined like this: Scissor can cut paper. Stone can crush scissors. Paper can wrap stone.

If there is a tie, try again. Instead of calling out "jan," "ken," "pon," say "*ai,*" "*kode,*" "*sho.*" This means "to toss again."

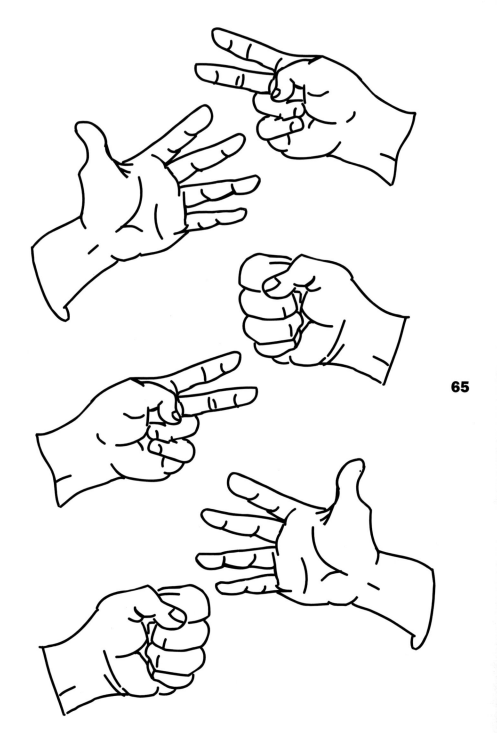

66

NATSU
SUMMER

67

Photo: Keith Nakata

OBON, A Gathering of JOY

The temple parking lot is a burst of white and airy softness. Hundreds of strung *chōchin* radiate out from the wooden *yagura,* their paper tails softly fluttering in the early evening breeze. The *"monku-monku"* maintenance crew has been at work preparing the temple for the Obon celebration, setting up the wooden tower or yagura and stringing the lanterns and lights. Mr. Nakamura is finishing up drawing the huge concentric chalk circles on the asphalt — guides for the *bon odori* dancers.

Mia and Ryan's Mom and Dad have been helping out as well. Dad's putting out the last of the folding chairs and Mom is setting up the table for selling those last-minute raffle tickets.

"Oh, it's time to get ready. Come on you two, let's go upstairs and get dressed." Mom attempts to round up the kids.

Grabbing a paper shopping bag and a furoshiki bundle, Mom starts up the stairs with Mia and Ryan following behind. In the *tatami* room people are already getting dressed. Ryan pulls out his red *happi* from the furoshiki, puts it on over his T-shirt, grabs a *tenugui* and is finished.

"Bye, see ya," his words echo as he dashes away.

"Ryannnnnnn!," his mother calls. "Do you know where your *taiko* sticks are?"

obon
a Buddhist observance held annually in the summer months of July and August to honor the memory of the deceased. For many U.S. temples, the observance includes a memorial service, followed by *bon odori*. This very festive and lively observance is also an important fundraising opportunity for many temples who sponsor carnivals and other fundraising activities.

bon odori
dances performed at the temple as part of the Obon observance. Many of the dances developed out of a Buddhist context, others are folk dances from various geographic regions of Japan.

yagura
a raised platform or tower set up in the middle of the dance grounds.

chōchin
paper lanterns

"monku-monku"
a phrase meaning to complain

tatami
traditional Japanese floor mat made of rice straw

happi
short, loose-fitting Japanese coat

tenugui
rectangular cotton cloth used as a towel or head-covering; also an accessory in many Bon dances

69

Onegai-shimasu.
Please do this favor for me.

yukata
light cotton, summer kimono

obi
cloth sash

shibori
method of dyeing fabric; like tie-dye

geta
wooden clogs

kachi-kachi two pairs of bamboo sections used like castanets

kawaii
cute

chotto-matte
wait a minute

kanzashi
Japanese hair ornament

70

"Don't you have them?" he questions.

"I do," his mother said as she handed them to him, speaking slowly. "They're your responsibility, put them someplace where you can find them. So when it's time for you kids to play, you'll be ready."

"Yeah, yeah, yeah," his voice fades away as he runs down the stairs.

Mom notices Ryan has dropped his tenugui in his rush to escape any more words of warning. She starts to call him back, then shrugs and drapes the tenugui around her neck.

"Harada-san, *onegai-shimasu*," she says to one of the women nearby, "would you dress Mia for me, please."

Mia stands a little shyly as Mrs. Harada carefully unwraps the remains of the bundle. Unfolding a brightly colored *yukata* with pink and red flowers and a bright pink *shibori* sash, she ruffles through to check what else is included.

"O.K., Mia-chan, let's get you ready, too."

Within minutes, after some final adjustment in length, a few quick tugs and tucks, she is ready. *Geta* on her bare feet, *kachi-kachi* tucked into her obi, and tenugui draped across her shoulders, she starts for the door.

"*Kawaii, kawaii,*" all the adults chorus.

"*Chotto-matte,*" Mrs. Harada calls her back. She tucks the *uchiwa* or round fan into the big bow sash knotted at her back. And from a small square box, she brings out the *kanzashi* and attaches it to Mia's pony-tail.

Outside young and old, men and women begin to line up for the first dance. Guests from other temples have on their identical *happi* coats and form a contingent of purple or yellow or red. Teenagers sport happi over tank tops and big, baggy shorts. One temple "character" has his *yukata* hiked up to his underwear and has painted his face bright red.

"Welcome to our annual Obon celebration. Before we begin, let us all *gasshō.*" a voice on the microphone announces."

"*Namuamidabutsu, namuamidabutus, namuamidabutsu,*" everyone intones.

The scratches of the old recording proceed the music on the loudspeaker, the familiar restrains of the first song, "Bon Odori Uta" and the Bon Odori begins. The taiko beats out the rhythm and the dancers fill the circles. Mia follows behind her mother, imitating her movements, her arms and her feet struggle to keep up. The dance is flurry of familiar sound, colors, and motion.

gasshō
Buddhist gesture of the hands, made by placing palms together at chest level. A gesture of reverence and thanks.

taiko
Japanese wooden drum

Namuamidabutsu
"I take refuge in the Buddha Amida" An expression of receiving the Buddhist Truth in the Jodo Shinshu sect of Buddhism.

Getting **Ready** FOR **Obon**

Use the following words to label under the appropriate pictures:

yukata

uchiwa

chōchin

geta

kachi-kachi

zori

tenugui

obi

taiko

72

TANKŌ BUSHI
Coal Miner's SONG

tsu— ki ga de ta de ta tsu ki ga — de ta—
つ— き が で た で た つき が — で た —

yo i yoi mi i ke ta n kō — no u e ni — de
ヨ イ ヨ イ み い け た ん こ う — の — う え に — で

ta a n ma ri en to tsu — — ga ta ka
た あ ん ま り え ん と つ — — が た か

i — no de sa — zo ya o tsuki
い — の で さ — ぞ や お つき

sa n ke mu ta — ka ro sa no yoi yoi
さ ん け む た — か ろ サ ノ ヨ イ ヨ イ

For Japanese Americans, one of the most familiar and popular of Japanese folk songs is Tankō Bushi or the "Coal-Miner's Song." The simple, catchy melody and easy gestures have made this song and dance an enduring favorite.

73

Tsuki ga deta, deta

Tsuki ga deta, a yoi, yoi

Miike tankō no ue ni deta

Anmari entotsu ga takai node

Sazo ya otsukisan kemutakaro

Sa no yoi, yoi

Translation:

The moon is up, the moon is up *yoi, yoi.*

Up over the Miike coal mines, It's come up.

Wouldn't Old Man Moon be annoyed by the smoke?

When the chimney's so high, s*a no yoi, yoi.*

Making a CHŌCHIN

A chōchin is a paper lantern that often decorates the yagura and dancing area at Obon. Chōchin means "carrying lantern" and refers to a type of lantern carried by monks when they traveled at night.

A very simple chōchin can be made out of paper.

Materials:

pattern

scissors

glue

hole-punch

string

markers

Procedure:

Photo copy and cut out the pattern at right.

You can decorate or color the bands around the top of your chōchin if you wish.

Fold it in half length-wise. With scissors cut along the dotted lines, stopping at the solid lines.

When you have finished, unfold the paper and bring the "xxx" sides together, overlapping one side over the other and securing it in place with glue or paste.

With a hole punch, make two holes opposite each other at the marked circles.

Tie an 8-inch piece of string through each hole.

1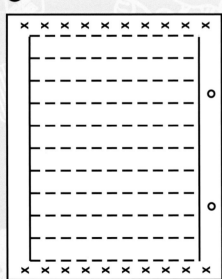

2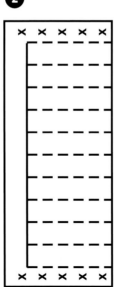

3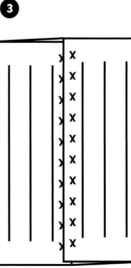

4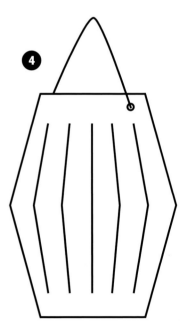

74

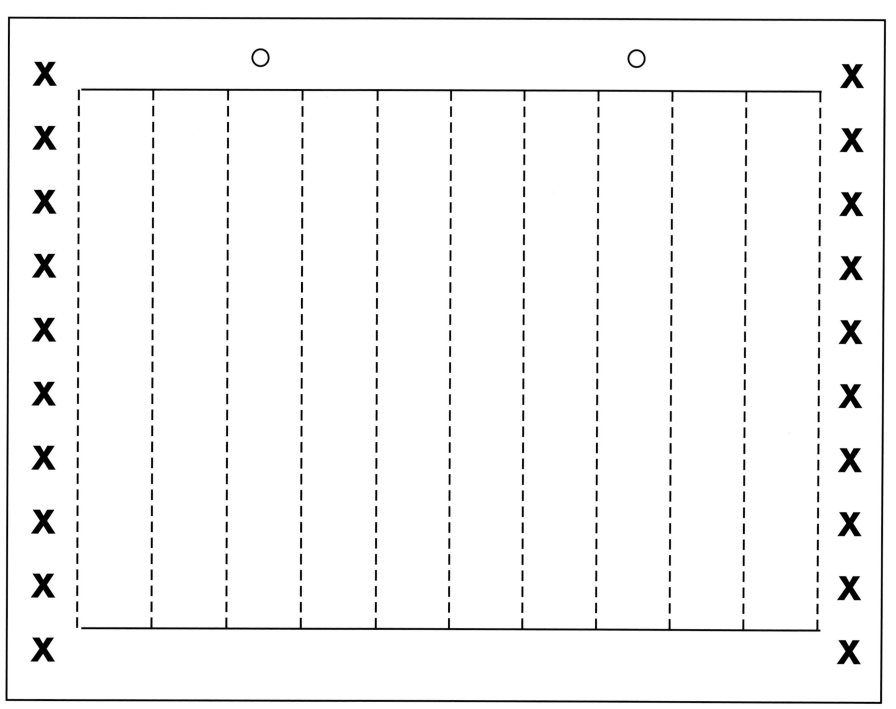

75

Furoshiki

A furoshiki is a large piece of square fabric used for wrapping and carrying things. In Japan, furoshiki are used every day by people for carrying everything from lunches to books, to groceries, to heavy bedding. In formal circumstances, gifts will be delivered wrapped in a furoshiki. There are many ways of tying a furoshiki. *Here* is one of the most common and simple.

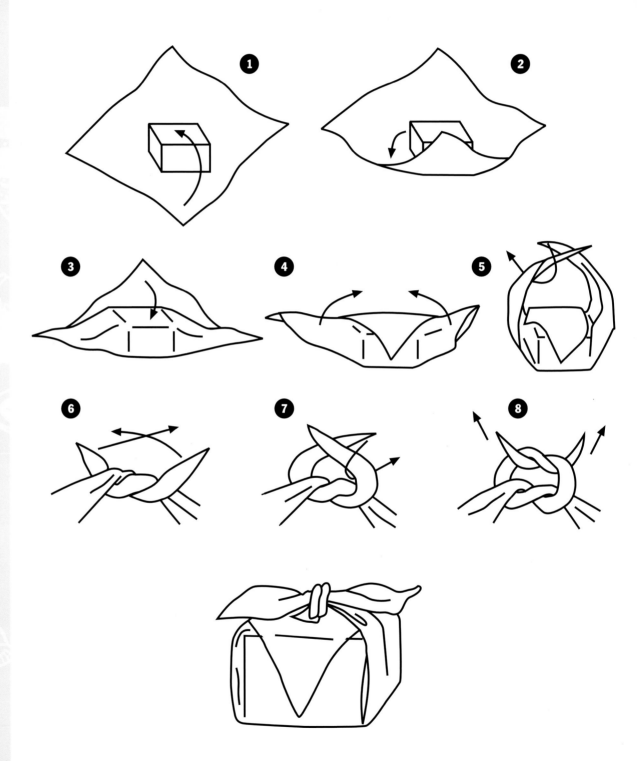

don kara don don kara don don DON
TAIKO

Taiko in Japanese means "large drum." The drum is a universal instrument found in every culture of the world and an important part of ritual, celebration, and daily life. According to taiko musician Johnny Mori, who performs and shares information with school children about the taiko, "in rural Japan the taiko was located in the center of the village, the boundaries of the village decided by the farmers ability to hear the sounding of the drum. The taiko communicated emergencies, important news, any need for the village to gather together."

In the U.S. new taiko forms developed from the desire of Japanese Americans to express and explore their Japanese heritage. Many taiko groups grew out of the activities of local Buddhist temples and community organizations. Taiko pieces have some direct roots to Japan and a style of drumming which is heard at *matsuri* or Japanese festivals; however, many U.S. taiko groups have created a very distinctive Japanese American style of play, drawing on the rhythms and patterns of other cultures and communities. Twenty-five years ago there were only a few taiko groups in the U.S. Today there are currently over eighty taiko groups throughout the country. Some of the groups are professional touring groups, but the majority of them play taiko as a means of self expression, exploring Japanese American culture, and supporting local community activities.

There are many different types of taiko, some of them are;

ōdaiko
large, tacked drum which is placed on a stand at chest level

josuke or chū taiko
a medium-sized tacked drum which is placed at a diagonal on a folding stand.

shimedaiko
a small drum, tacked or traditionally bound by ropes (or **shime**)

Accompanying the taiko are many percussive instruments and often a Japanese wind instrument, like a *fue* or *shakuhachi.*

Making your own TAIKO DRUM

Try making your own mini taiko drum. Then practice your taiko drumming at home.

Large wooden hashi or chopsticks can serve as bachi or drum sticks.

Materials:

5# empty coffee can

2 large brown grocery bags (12"x 17")

white glue

twine (approximately 42" in length)

paint brush (medium)

water (approximately 24 oz. in a fairly large-sized container)

can opener

scissors

compass

tape measure

ruler

pencil

newspaper

one large rubber band

Procedure:

Use the can opener to remove the bottom of the coffee can. Careful, the can edge may be sharp.

Using the scissors, cut along a side seam of one of the paper bags to the bottom edge of the bag. Continue to cut along the bottom section until you have cut away the bottom of the bag. You now have a large flat piece of paper.

Repeat this procedure on your second bag as well.

Take one of your opened up bags. From your large piece of paper you will cut out a long piece of paper that will wrap completely around the outside face of your can, overlapping approximately 2 inches. This piece will measure approximately 7" x 22". (Use your tape measure to confirm the measurement of your can.) With your pencil and ruler, mark the proper dimensions on your paper and cut out.

Now take the second bag. You are going to draw two circles the circumference of your can, plus 2 inches. The easiest way to do this is to place your can on the brown paper and trace along the circumference of your can. Using the compass, extend the diameter 2 inches. Cut out the two circles. These will become the top of your drum.

Spread some newspaper, the next part is messy.

Crumble up your long piece of paper. Open up and dip the paper briefly into the bowl of water. Squeeze out the excess. Brush glue onto the outside of the can. Carefully wrap the paper around the sides of the can. With your brush, spread glue thoroughly over the wrapped can. Use the glue generously. When it dries it will make a nice strong surface. You can also tear small leftover pieces from the bags (approximately 3 inches in length). Wet them and then overlay them, one by one randomly onto your can. This gives the surface a more "earthy" look. Be sure to glue over all pieces of paper you apply.

With your two cut-out circles, crumble up each one. Open them up and dip one circle into the water. Stretch the circle across the top of the can. Brush glue on generously. Take the second circle and dip it into the water and lay it across the first circle. Use a rubber band to secure the circles to the can. Continue to brush glue generously over the circles and touch-up any areas along the sides.

Set aside your drum to dry. After the drum is dry, remove the rubber band. Take your length of twine and wrap it around the top of your drum.

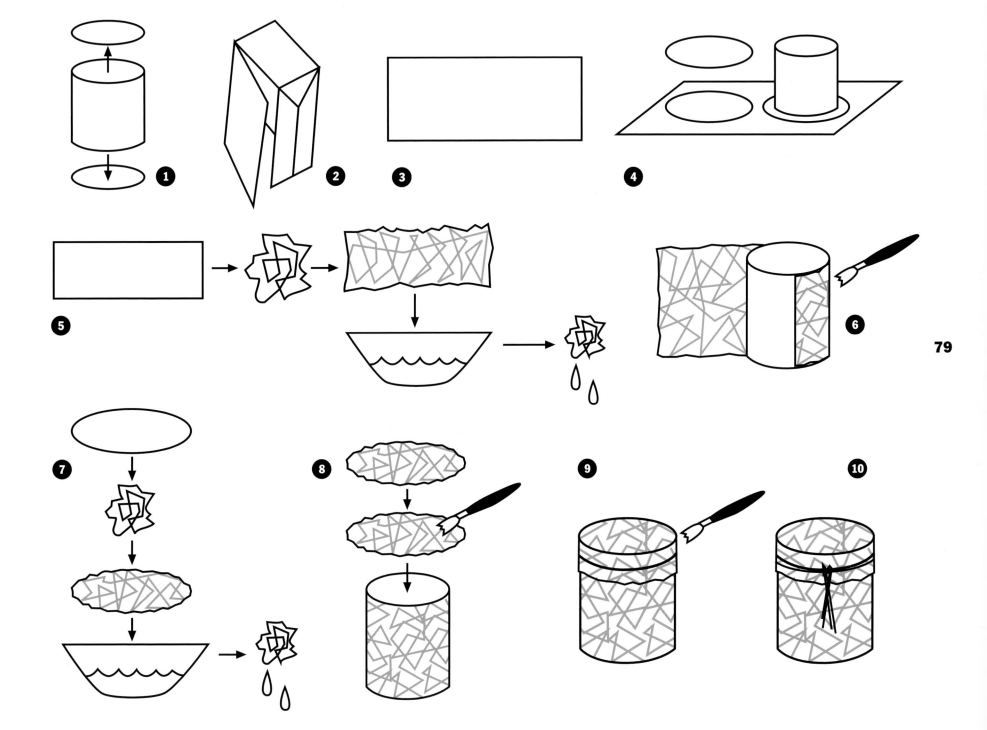

NISEI WEEK JAPANESE Festival

One of the oldest Japanese American festivals is the annual Nisei Week Japanese Festival in Los Angeles's Little Tokyo. The first festival was held in 1934. The Little Tokyo community wanted to promote local businesses and present the traditional and cultural arts of the Japanese American community. Except for a seven year interruption caused by World War II, the Los Angeles Nisei Week has provided generations of Japanese Americans an opportunity to celebrate and share their cultural heritage and community interests.

A full calendar of events held each August make up the Nisei Week Festival, including the Annual Nisei Week Parade through the streets of Little Tokyo led by a host of Japanese dancers, followed by marching bands, floats and the debut of the Nisei Week Queen and her Court. Exhibits and demonstrations throughout the downtown area display the traditional arts, like; *ikebana* (flower arrangement), *bonsai* (miniature trees), shodō (calligraphy), doll-making, and ceramics as well as demonstrate a variety of traditional martial arts forms, like; *kendō*, *judō*, *aikidō* and *karate*. A favorite attraction is the annual Carnival where an array of Japanese and American food can be sampled, where anyone can try their luck at a variety of carnival games, and everyone bumps into friends, neighbors, and relatives.

In California, Nisei Week is one of the largest Japanese American festivals and extends over several weeks. Summer is also the time when many of the local Japanese American community centers and churches sponsor festivals featuring displays/exhibits, food booths, games and folk dancing. Many of the Buddhist temples combine their Obon celebration with a carnival, food-faire and cultural exhibits. Throughout the U.S. where there are large concentrations of Japanese Americans, similar festivals and Obon celebrations are held during the summer.. In San Francisco's Japantown, it is called the Nihonmachi Street Fair. San Jose hosts the Nikkei Matsuri and the Seattle Obon is one of the big summer events of the city.

Photos Courtesy of Nisei Week Japanese Festival and the Toyo Miyatake Studio

What is your FAVORITE CARNIVAL FOOD?

```
C U J G V L G K L U F G T I D
O H D F W J K U R I M A N J U
R W I A T N P H O T D O G I P
N Q E C N W U P R T Y U H I O
O S C A K G D S O D A S G H J
N N H Y I E O K L P A A K O L
T O A A N G N S E R C N E B C
H W S K T A O T I N L O L D K
E C U I O N K H E O H N R S A
C O B S K G C L N R Y E H N T
O N A O I S A E D I I B E K Y
B E O B A M D A D M N Y G I N
S T E A A O B T O A C H A R Y
E N A T R E S K C K S R F K J
Y D E A R I N A R I Z U S H I
```

inarizushi

tamale

norimaki

oden

udon

yakisoba

chicken teriyaki

chirashi

snow cone

kintoki

hot dog

dango

soda

kurimanju

chasu bao

corn on the cob

popcorn

81

See page 116 for answers

82

Photo: Hirokazu Kosaka

MIKAWAYA
a Japanese Confectionery

How long has Mikawaya been operating in Little Tokyo?

Our family has operated our confectionery store in Little Tokyo for over 85 years. Mikawa is a town in Aichi-ken, Japan, that's where our family is from. That's why our store is called Mikawa-ya. "*Ya*" means shop or store in Japanese.

What kinds of things do you make at Mikawaya and how did you learn to make them?

I learned the business through experience. As soon as we were old enough we would help in the store, especially around the holidays. Oshōgatsu is our busiest time of year because people have to have their mochi. The last few days of December we practically work around the clock because local people want their mochi as fresh as possible.

At Mikawaya we also produce a variety of Japanese sweets. These are generally called *wagashi* and include a variety of Japanese pastries. Japanese Americans more commonly will call these sweets *manjū*. Some are made of mochi flour and can be filled with a sweet bean paste, others are more like a baked dough with a sweet bean filling.

Are there special occasions for manjū?

Different kinds of Japanese sweets are traditionally associated with different occasions. For Buddhist funerals it was traditional to make an offering for the deceased of a simple, white manju. A *kiku* or chrysanthemum is stamped on the outside of the manju and inside there is dark *an* filling or bean-paste made from azuki beans. Nowadays people tend to order a variety of *mochi-gashi* for funerals. I think this is because after the service, families serve the manjū and so they select a variety people will enjoy eating.

Certain other mochigashi are associated with other events and holidays. For weddings, couples will sometimes order a white and pink manju with a *tsuru-kame* (crane and turtle) stamped on it. The tsuru-kame is a felicitous symbol of long life, popular at weddings and other happy occasions. For Boy's Day we make a *kashiwa-mochi* or manjū wrapped in an oak-leaf (the oak symbolizing strength). The *sakura-mochi* or manjū wrapped in a cherry blossom leaf as well as a tri-colored (white, green and pink) mochigashi are associated with Girl's Day.

I think here in the United States we sell a greater variety of wagashi. In Japan certain areas would have its regional specialties and serve a more limited selection. A favorite here in L.A. and Hawaii is the manjū that looks like a potato. You may not see that one selling in the more "high-tone" shops in Japan because it's a fairly simple, not a fancy sweet. But here in the U.S., we eat what we like.

Do young Japanese Americans like Sansei and Yonsei like manjū?

The younger people seem to prefer the manjū without the fillings, like the pink and white striped one, or the orange-flavored square one. And now we have mochi ice-cream. We've developed a dessert with a mochi outside and ice-cream center. It comes in a variety of flavors and is really popular. And at Mikawaya we do make one of the best snow-cones in town.

What will be the future for Mikawaya?

I feel pretty strongly that we are in the business of maintaining Japanese traditions, and we'll continue to make all our different varieties of wagashi for the community.

And I feel certain there will be a place for us, people still have to have their mochi for Oshōgatsu.

Maneki NEKO

Perched on a shelf or counter-top in many of the Little Tokyo shops or restaurants is a cute ceramic or papier mache cat, sitting on his haunches waving "hello" with his paw. This "good-luck" cat is called *maneki neko*. According to 17th century legend, there was a cat named Tama who lived in a very poor Buddhist temple. One day a traveling lord and his retinue noticed the cat sitting on the steps of the temple. The cat appeared to be waving to the lord to stop and come in. Curious, the lord decided to stop and rest at the temple. At the temple, the Lord encountered the temple priest and was so impressed by this experience that he decided to become a patron of the temple, giving money to improve and refurbish it. Over the years Tama the cat has become a symbol of good luck — inviting good fortune and wealth.

84

Interview with REV. KENSHO Furuya

Rev. Kensho Furuya is a 6th dan Black Belt in Aikidō and the Chief Instructor of the Aikidō Center of Los Angeles and the Los Angeles Sword and Swordsmanship Society. He teaches Japanese martial arts and Japanese culture in a traditional Japanese-style *dōjō* or school he built with his students in a 100 year-old warehouse in Little Tokyo.

Rev. Furuya coordinates the annual Nisei Week Martial Arts Festival and the Spring Festival Asian Pacific Martial Arts Festival, presenting master teachers from a variety of martial arts schools.

Tell us about yourself and your introduction to martial arts.

I am a *Sansei* from the Pasadena area born in 1948. I began studying *aikidō* and *kendō* when I was about ten years old at the Chūō Dōjō in East Los Angeles. I studied alongside both my father and grandfather and I really enjoyed the fellowship and community aspect of learning with them at the community center. We were part of a community. We participated in the other activities of the Center, like Obon, picnics, and Japanese school events. This is very different than learning martial arts as it is often taught today. A dōjō separate and unconnected to a community is a very different experience.

What is the benefit of studying a martial art?

Well of course, if you study any martial art or self-defense form you will probably become stronger and be better able to defend yourself physically. With an art like aikidō you develop greater flexibility of motion and better balance. You feel more centered and a sense of well-being and energy. My students tell me that practice has all kinds of benefits in every area of their lives — from improved family life to better ability to concentrate on schoolwork or job. In our dōjō you learn about Japanese culture and the old samurai way of life. Before and after practice, everyone must clean the mats just like in the old-style dōjō in Japan over 100 years ago. Everyone must learn how to bow to each other before and after practice. In Japanese this is called *reigi-saho* or etiquette. This builds self-confidence, but humility

85

and modesty at the same time. It is said that this is the basis of all traditional Japanese martial arts.

How would you describe aikidō?

Aikidō's roots go back to ancient Japan, but its present-day form was created by its founder Morihei Ueshiba in the 1920's. Aikidō is based on joint locks and throws rather than punches and kicks. There is no competition in aikidō, no sparring or matches. Although some movements are very "soft," many movements are very fast. More than any other art, aikidō is most often used by law-enforcement officers all over the world. Aikidō techniques are very effective, rather simple to learn and you don't have to injure your opponent to control him.

What should new students consider when they want to begin studying a martial art?

New students should first choose whichever art appeals to them most; seems to suit their personality, physical level and personal goals most comfortably. Once you know which art you want to pursue, the next task is to find the best school and instructor you can possibly find. Don't use cost and convenience as your standard. Don't think that a teacher is good because the tuition is cheaper and he is closer to your home. If you have to drive a few more miles and pay a few extra dollars, it is always worth it in the long run to study under the most qualified teacher you can find. Next, go with an empty mind. Don't make your expectations too high and understand that it will take a few months before you begin to see the results of your training. Finally, a good way to evaluate the teacher is to look at his students — their level of skill and how they act on and off the mats. A good school is always clean and in good order. A good teacher will never make foolish promises to you.

Photo: Larry Armstrong

MUSUBI or n i g i r i

The *nigiri* is a portable version of a rice meal. Especially during the warm weather of summer when families can picnic at the park or beach and when there is an abundance of carnivals and festivals, nigiri are favorite ways to eat rice. The most common rice "ball" is the *nori musubi* — a ball or triangle or egg-shaped cupful of cooked rice wrapped in a square of seaweed. Often something tasty is placed in the center of a nigiri, like a pickled plum, called an *umeboshi*.

Rice or *kome* is the staple of the Japanese diet. While bread and potatoes are important to an European or American meal, rice is the core of the Japanese meal. In fact, the Japanese words for cooked rice, *meshi* or *gohan* have come to mean, the meal itself.

Making a MUSUBI

Materials:

Pot of cooked rice or gohan

Shamoji or wooden (or plastic) rice paddle

Salt, optional

Umeboshi (salted plum) optional

Nori or dried sea-weed

Bowl of water

Procedure:

After the rice is cooked and steamed for a few minutes, turn the rice with the shamoji (digging down to the bottom, bringing up a scoopful of rice and turning it over) This helps the rice to cool evenly.

When the gohan is still hot, but cooled enough so that it can be handled, you can begin.

Wet your hands. Salt them lightly, if you wish.

Scoop out approximately one cupful of rice. (Your musubi, however, can be as large or as small as you wish)

To make a triangular-shaped musubi, hold the rice lightly in one hand (palm up) and place the other hand on top. (illustration)

Using a light squeezing motion of both hands, your hands will form a triangular shape.

As your rice is taking shape, flip the triangle in your hands so that you are compressing the rice on all sides.

Do not squeeze too hard, or too lightly. (Practice makes perfect. You do not want your musubi to be so lightly packed that it falls apart when you eat it, or so over-handled it becomes pasty.

Hint: If the rice is just getting everywhere, you need to wet your hands again.

Variations: Try putting something in the center, a piece of fish, an umeboshi, seasoned seaweed.

Frustrated? If you are having difficulty, you can also purchase many inexpensive plastic or wooden molds that will easily make your nigiri.

89

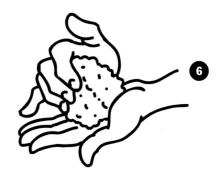

OMIYAGE

The Japanese word for gift is _miyage._ The Japanese love to give gifts, not just for the customary important occasions, like weddings, birthdays, anniversaries, graduations, but for almost every social occasion. In Japan there are two important gift-giving seasons: during the summer (_ochūgen_); and at the end of the year (_oseibo_). At these times gifts are given to express gratitude and appreciation. Not just a social custom, gift-giving underscores the importance of mutual help and interdependence.

Japanese Americans continue the custom of constant gift-giving, but without as much formality nor the extremes of the Japanese. Still Japanese Americans have difficulty visiting anyone "empty-handed" and feel the "need" to reciprocate with a gift after receiving one. A small gift expresses appreciation to our teachers, ministers, neighbors, and friends.

In the summertime, life is less hectic and families have time to visit friends, go on outings and take vacations. Visiting friends or relations usually means a gift, maybe of food or something to drink. When traveling, buying souvenirs for friends and family is an important part of the itinerary.

Making WRAPPING PAPER

This is a very simple way to make your own wrapping paper based on traditional Japanese paper-dyeing techniques. It's easy and results are always good. After you've tried the techniques below, come up with your own way to fold the paper. Experiment. You'll be pleased with the results.

Materials:

*3 or 4 liquid tempera paints of different colors

paper (Rice paper works best, but other absorbent papers, like-newsprint will work.) Tissue paper will work, too.

3 or 4 containers for the paint (old tofu containers, plastic bowls, etc.)

newspaper

*Note: For the most brilliant colors, liquid dyes work best, but they will stain your fingers and clothes.

Procedure:

Spread the newspaper to protect your table or workplace.

Pour paint into containers; fill to approximately one-inch in depth. (Paint should be runny, not too thick.)

Basic Paper Fold:

Using your paper horizontally; make an approximate fold of 1-1/2 inch.

Using this fold as a guide, proceed to pleat your entire piece of paper like a fan.

Without unfolding your paper, now make a fold at one end of approximately 2 inches.

Now proceed to pleat back and forth again, until

your paper is a small folded rectangle.

You are now ready to dip your paper into the paint.

Select your first color and dip one corner of your folded paper into the paint (for about 5 seconds.)

Select another color and a second corner.

Continue until you have dipped each corner. You can even go back and re-dip just the tip of one corner into a second color.

When you are finished, carefully unfold your paper and see the results.

Let it dry on a sheet of newspaper.

Hints:

If you are using tissue paper, do not allow the paper to sit in the paint too long or it will easily tear.

You can put rubber bands on your folded paper before you dip into paint to hold it more securely.

Experiment on how you dip into the paint and how you fold. Rather than corners, you can dip entire sides of your rectangle. Or after you have pleated your fan, instead of a rectangle fold, you can attempt a triangular fold, like this...

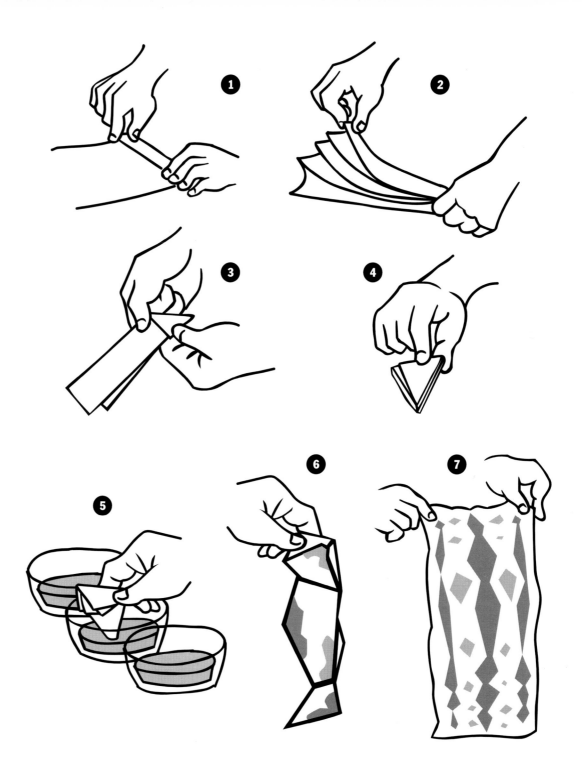

TANABATA, or Hoshimatsuri

is a popular summer festival in Japan. It is also called *Hoshimatsuri* or the Star Festival and is celebrated each year on July 7. The festival begins with an old Chinese legend about two stars; known in the West as Verda and Altair.

Long, long ago in the heavenly skies lived Princess Shokujo (Verda star) who was a skillful weaver. One day she met and fell in love with a handsome herder, Kengyū (Altair star). The two wanted very much to marry, and after much pleading, the king finally gave his consent. Shokujo and Kengyū were so much in love that they neglected their responsibilities and duties — Shokujo her weaving and Kengyū taking care of his herd. Angered, the king decided to separate the two lovers and placed them on opposite sides of the *Amanogawa* (Milky Way). The only time the two are allowed to meet is once a year on the 7th day of the 7th month. On that night, magpies form a bridge with their outstretched wings and allow the couple to cross over and come together.

Tanabata is a national holiday in Japan and traditionally of interest to young girls. Weaving was once of primary importance to the Japanese household and the duty of women. Young women also identified with the romantic story and their own hope for success in love. Tanabata is celebrated with special foods and the writing of poems. Poems are written on sheets of paper and tied to bamboo branches, along with folded cranes. Another popular decoration is the *kusudama* or colorful paper balls with paper blossoms.

HAIKU, a JAPANESE Poem

One type of Japanese poem is called the *haiku*. The haiku has 17 syllables, arranged in three lines of five, seven and five syllables. The haiku traditionally deals with nature. There is usually a seasonal word in every haiku — referring to a plant, animal or an activity which evokes an image of a particular season. The following haiku written by Issa Kobayashi (1763-1827) is a good illustration:

Opening their mouths
They await the parent birds
In the autumn rain

Kuchi akate
oya matsu tori ya
aki no ame

The following group of haiku include one written by the late Rev. H. John Yamashita, who served many years at Centenary United Methodist Church in Los Angeles. His two granddaughters, Lucy and Mary Jane Boltz follow their grandfather's interest and also write haiku.

"Shapes in the Sky"
by Hiroshi John Yamashita

Clouds dancing lazily
    After each other
        Changing shapes each moment

"Spring"
by Lucy Asako Boltz

Everything is new.
That is why I like Spring and
May is my birthday

"Fall"
by Mary Jane Tomi Boltz

Lightly falling leaves,
Strong gusts of wind blowing past.
Time for warm jackets.

Writing a HAIKU

Write your own haiku with five syllables in the first line, seven syllables in the second and five syllables at the end, for a total of 17 syllables. Remember to include a word which describes one of the four seasons.

TITLE _____

First line: five (5) syllables _____

Second line: seven (7) syllables _____

End: five (5) syllables _____

TITLE _____

First line: five (5) syllables _____

Second line: seven (7) syllables _____

End: five (5) syllables _____

Total: seventeen (17) syllables

AKI
AUTUMN

Grandma's HOUSE

My grandmother's house is like our house, but more cozy. And she has lots of Japanese things in her house. When we sleep over she puts out the foam pad and spreads out the big *futon*. It's very soft and has pretty flowers all over. But it's so hot! When I lie under it, I feel like I can't breathe.

noren

zabuton

bonsai

futon

MY Grandparents' HOUSE

The mini-van turned up the familiar streets to Grandma and Grandpa's house. Mia sat upright, anticipating Grandpa's figure, hunched over the flower beds or clipping the already trim hedges with his shears. There he was...hosing the driveway off, washing away the traces of freshly edged lawn.

"Hi Grandpa," she and Ryan yelled out as they slammed the car door.

"We're spending the night, you know. We brought tapes to watch later and cookies for dessert," Mia informed as she struggled with her bag up the porch stairs.

Grandma was in the kitchen, bustling about expertly; setting the table, draining the steamed broccoli and turning the hot *gohan* with the *shamoji.*

"Hi," she said without stopping her work. "Mia and Ryan, help Grandma set the table. Take out the forks and ohashi, and bring out the milk. Mia, get the *zabuton* from the dining room so you can be higher when you sit down."

The children added things to an already full kitchen table. Dinner was always in the kitchen, only on holidays did they eat in the dining room. The table was always covered anyways, of paper

gohan
cooked rice

shamoji
wooden rice paddle; used for turning the cooked rice and serving

zabuton
a cushion used for sitting on, approximately 20 inches square.

99

kiku
chrysanthemum; a favorite flower of the Japanese; symbol of the Imperial Family; and, associated with the fall season.

kanreki
60th birthday celebration. An important birthday in Japanese tradition as it indicates the completion of one life cycle.

tonkatsu
pork cutlet, dipped in bread-crumbs and deep-fried

mayonnaise and shoyu
a popular dip for most steamed green vegetables, i.e., green beans, asparagus, zucchini.

nasu with miso
an eggplant dish prepared with soybean paste

tsukemono
pickled vegetables

nabe
Japanese pot

yūdōfu
tofu or bean-curd cake, warmed in a light broth

stacks, magazines and Grandma's latest craft project. For a while she was making artificial flowers out of discarded plastic six-pack soda rings. After carefully cutting, shaping, and spray-painting, the finished *kiku* belied any link to their origins. Grandma and her sisters made over 200 flowers last year for Uncle Roy's *kanreki* or 60th birthday celebration. Her current project was crocheting long strips of cut-up plastic grocery bags transforming them into tote bags of incredible durability.

Grandma surveyed the table, "Ryan go tell Grandpa it's time to eat, and both of you go and wash your hands."

They sat down to a table of *tonkatsu*, steamed broccoli (with a mayonnaise and shoyu dip), grilled *nasu* with *miso*, gohan, and a small dish of *tsukemono*. At the center of the table was a round cast-iron nabe sitting on a little hot plate.

"Ooo, what's that..." Mia looked inside.

"*Yūdōfu*, try it, you'll like it. See, it's just warm *tōfu*, you both like.

"Take it out like this and dip it in this sauce," she demonstrated and plopped a piece in her mouth.

"Not for me," Ryan insisted. "And none of that eggplant stuff. Where's the Bulldog sauce?"

"Just try a little." Grandpa insisted.

"I'll try it Grandpa," Mia offered.

"Itadakimasu," Grandma reminded.

"Itadakimasu," everyone repeated.

Mia ate contentedly. This was the best! She watched Grandma and Grandpa catch chunks of *tōfu* with a flat wire spoon. Dipping into a sauce of shoyu, grated *daikon* and lemon, they ate with relish. It looked good.

"Mmmm, Ryan, it's good," Mia announced as she swallowed the warm, soft *tōfu*.

"See, I told you," Grandpa reminded. "We made this last week-end when Auntie Sandy and her new boyfriend came over. Boy, they ate it up. That guy can eat! No *enryo*, huh Mama."

"That's o.k., that's o.k. That's what I like to see," Grandma smiled."

Soon too many hands were competing for the last few bites. It was good, Ryan had to agree. But he still wasn't going to eat any eggplant!

"Gochisōsama," Grandpa said with a sigh. "That was good." He looked at the little bit of gohan left in his chawan and the little bit of tsukemono in the dish. "Maybe, I have room for a little *ochazuke, mottainai kara*" he said reaching for the tea.

Bulldog Sauce
referring to a brand name of a commercially-made Japanese sauce (a Bulldog pictured on the label) served with tonkatsu.

chazuke
gohan with ocha or hot tea poured over the top. A snack or the final finish to a meal, tsukemono is usually eaten with chazuke.

mottainai
wasteful

enryo

to use restraint

NOREN

A *noren* is a short cloth curtain hung across an entry or doorway. It is commonly draped at the entrance of Japanese shops and restaurants, but is also found extended across the doorways of kitchens or other rooms in a Japanese home. A noren across the door of a business will often have the name of the shop and/or its *mon* (trademark).

A typical noren is made from cotton cloth dyed a deep indigo blue and is slit in two places so that people can easily enter. A design or *kanji* (Chinese characters) printed in white is commonly the second color. Often the designs are simple geometric shapes, or motifs from nature, like leaves, flowers, bamboo, etc.

102

Making a NOREN

Materials:

3 sheets of dark blue construction paper or colored paper, 10"x15"

4 strips of the same paper cut to 1-1/4"x6"

3/4" masking tape

white glue

markers

*sponges

white liquid tempera

ruler

pencil

newspaper

(*Compressed sponges can be purchased at craft stores and cut into different shapes with scissors. They expand when wet with water.)

Procedure:

Spread newspaper onto the table or work surface

Align your 3 sheets of paper to make one long rectangle, with barely a space separating them.

Cut 2 pieces of masking tape, about 5", and tape the first sheet to the second, lining the tape with the top edge of the two sheets of paper Then tape the second sheet to the third sheet.

Measure 3/4" and mark with a pencil across the length of the three sheets of paper. Fold the paper on this line, covering over the masking tape. You may also glue lightly to secure. (This becomes the reverse side of our noren.)

Take your 4 small strips of paper and fold in half. Open up. Putting glue on one end of each strip, attach the strip to the top of the noren as shown, approximately 1" from the top of the paper. When the glue is dry, flip the noren over, re-fold the strips on the fold line and glue the remaining end of the strip to the back of the noren.

To imitate a stitched pattern, use a marker and duplicate the pattern shown on the four small strips.

Trace a simple design onto your sponge. Cut-out and dip into water. Wring out any excess.

Dip the flat surface of your sponge into

the white tempera and print your design on to your noren. (Remember Japanese designs are often simple. Limit yourself to one, two, maybe three sponges.)

When dry you can run a dowel or piece of bamboo through your noren. It's ready to hang.

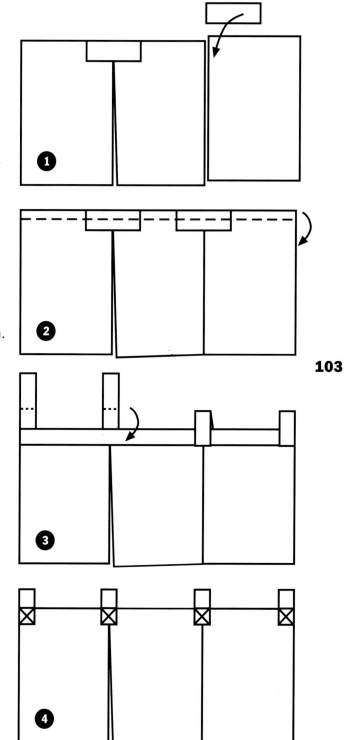

103

The Taste of TŌFU

The Chinese say that *tōfu* is the taste of a hundred things. It can be boiled, broiled, baked, fried, steamed, marinated, dried, frozen, and eaten fresh. Made of soybeans and full of proteins, tōfu is nutritious and inexpensive.

According to William Shurtleff of the Soyfoods Center, in 220 A.D. archeologists unearthed a description that suggests tōfu was made in northern China as early as the Eastern/Later Han Period. In Japan, tōfu was mentioned in the 12th century diary of a Shinto priest, Hiroshige Nakaomi, who placed tōfu on the altar as an offering.

Two popular Japanese tōfu dishes are *hiyayakko* in the summertime and yūdōfu in the winter. Hiyayakko is a chilled block of tōfu served with grated ginger, or *shoga,* and chopped green onions, topped with *katsuo bushi* or dried bonito shavings. For yūdōfu, cubed tōfu is warmed in a pot of heated water (with piece of dried *konbu* or seaweed added). The tōfu is eaten with shōyu or dipped in a shōyu-based dipping sauce. At a Japanese American potluck, look for tōfu salad, tōfu turkey casserole and tōfu spinach dip.

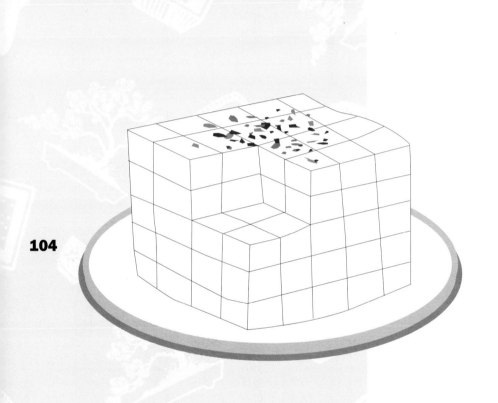

WASTE NOT, want not
MOTTAINAI

means wasteful and reflects an attitude characteristic of Japanese and Japanese Americans. A Buddhist term, mottainai refers to the principle that nothing exists alone, but all things are the result of various causes and conditions. To realize this connection is to have a sense of appreciation and responsibility for each other. In nature, we observe that nothing is wasted, but everything is recycled.

In daily life the concept of mottainai has come to mean a hesitancy to waste or throw anything away. Japanese Americans, especially the Issei and Nisei generation, are primary examples of upholding the "don't be mottainai" principle. Japanese Americans polled contributed the following examples of recycling, re-using and saving:

I save old calendars and use them as book covers.

I save old wrapping paper and use it to line my drawers.

I take two gallon plastic water bottles, cut off the tops and use them as disposable containers for food. One serves as the bottom and the other creates a cover.

I made a birdhouse out of discarded *kamaboko* (fish-cake) boards.

I save tōfu containers and use them to plant seedlings.

My Bāchan saved odds and ends of yarn and made beautiful afghans.

Japanese DISHES and KITCHEN Tools

Can you identify the following and tell how they are used:

owan
soup bowl

chawan
rice bowl

hashi-oki
chopstick rest

donburi
deep bowl

nabe
pot

suribachi
mortar

maki-su
screen for making sushi

oroshi
grater

106

SENSHIN Buddhist Temple Fujinkai
QUICK TAKUAN Recipe

Ingredients:

4 large daikon – peeled and sliced into 1/4 quarter-inch circles

2 Cups sugar

1/4 C salt

1/2 C vinegar

1 Tbl. whiskey (optional)

1 tsp Ajinomoto (optional)

Few drops of yellow food color

Mix all together. Let sit at room temperature until all sugar is dissolved. Pack into clean jars and refrigerate. *Takuan* is ready to eat in one or two days.

MARION MANAKA'S
easy CUCUMBER Tsukemono Recipe

Ingredients

6-8 pickling cucumbers

2 Cups water

2 Tbl salt

2 Tbl sugar

1 Tbl minced shoga

1 tsp minced garlic

1 tsp crushed red chili

Wash cucumbers and slice into quarter spears lengthwise. Pack in clean jar, pour above mixture over cucumbers and leave out at least 5 hours, then refrigerate.

Tsukemono

Tsukemono literally means "soaked things" and refers to Japanese pickled vegetables. Tsukemono is an important side dish to the Japanese meal. There are endless varieties of tsukemono depending on the seasoning base used and the particular region the tsukemono originates from. Some of the most popular tsukemono are *umeboshi*, *takuan* and *cucumber tsukemono.*

According to legend, takuan was invented by a Zen priest named Takuan Zenji who often went into the mountains alone to meditate for long periods of time. To sustain himself he would take a pot of cooking rice and a large *daikon* or Japanese radish with him. Takuan figured out a way to preserve the daikon with salt so that it would not spoil. The results were so popular that the preserved daikon was named after him. Incidentally, Takuan is the very same priest master-swordsman who was the teacher of the famous samurai, Miyamoto Musashi.

YES, No, Maybe so... ENRYO
By Rev. Masao KODANI

The definition of *Enryo* is found in the 15th book of the *Analects of Confucius:* "If a man takes no thought of distant things, he will unfailingly have regrets close at hand." In Japanese, the characters for "thought of distant things" is read "enryo". Used as a noun or a verb, it has come to mean simply "thinking deeply before acting". In short, if you do not think deeply before speaking or acting, you will have immediate regrets.

The Buddhists have clarified the point further by adding that if what you are about to say or do is based upon the Three Poisons, then do not act. The Three Poisons are Anger, Greed, and Ignorance. Given these two definitions and a bit of self-reflective honesty, we would have to keep our mouths shut and be immobile 90% of our walking lives. This is precisely what Enryo tries to get us to do. Indeed we have taken this advice so closely to heart that we are often called "the quiet people".

Though very much different from American logic, the logic of Enryo is this: The more reflective you are about the consequences of what you are about to say or do, the more you will avoid regrets and sorrow. Being quiet allows you to think on a deeper level than that of your ego alone. When one is quiet, one can truly listen, and when one truly listens, one can truly learn. Raising ones hand in a classroom at the slightest encouragement is most often not the result of an eager student wanting to know as it is an eager person wanting to show-off and impress. Listen first and ask your real questions later — do not intrude on the time of the other students. This is practicing the Silver Rule of Confucius — "Do **not** do unto others, what you would **not** have them do unto you". This is similar to the Golden Rule of the West — "**Do** unto others as you would have them **do** unto you", but greatly different in attitude. The former wishes to mind its own business, the latter to mind the business of us all. This is perhaps one of the reasons why Japanese Americans feel more comfortable asking questions privately after class. I do not know that it is so much the fear of making a fool of oneself in public as it is not wanting to be intrusive on others.

This Enryo has an enormous influence on us, from not touching the last piece of chashu on a plate to taking half an hour to decide by inferred consensus where to go to eat after a meeting.

In short, enryo is that body of restraints which disciplines us into learning to be more considerate of others and to put reins on our normally rampant egos. Letting it all hang out and speaking our mind whenever and wherever we please is self-indulgent, self-righteous ego tripping. Not to Enryo is simply put — "barbaric". Though some Japanese Americans look upon Enryo as the contrary, we continue to teach and practice it in our temples. Because it helps us to think on a deeper level than normal, and because it helps us to be more honest and considerate of others, there should be no Enryo in practicing and valuing Enryo.

KANREKI, The Big 6-0

According to Japanese tradition, when a person reaches his 60th birthday he has completed one complete life cycle and now begins a "second childhood."

This calculation is based on two sets of Chinese zodiac; the twelve animal years and the five elements (wood, fire, earth, metal and water). Each year is made up of a combination of both sets, for example; "fire-tiger." On the 60th year of a person's life he/she will return to the exact same animal and element symbol of one's birth.

The 60th birthday is an occasion for celebration. Traditionally the celebrant dresses in red clothes and a red cap, the customary colors for newborn babies. Friends and family are invited to a big party. Japanese Americans continue the observance of the kanreki, celebrating with a big party for friends and family. Often 1,000 cranes or senbazuru will be folded and displayed as a decoration and symbol of good health. The particular animal year of the birthday person will also be a popular theme.

The other important birthdays are: the 42nd year, 70th, 77th, 80th, 88th, and 90th. The 42nd year marks the beginning of the decline of the body and the beginning of maturity, skill and beauty. The 88th is another major celebration, like the kanreki.

In Asian tradition, the elderly are valued for their experience and maturity. The Japanese word for teacher, *Sensei*, literally means "those who have lived before us," implying our elders are our teachers.

Taking an ORAL History

Everyone has important stories. History is not just about the famous and newsworthy, but the story of ordinary people. Too often, the stories of ethnic communities, like the Japanese American community is left out or too briefly told in history books and other sources. Knowing one's history provides an understanding of the past and a key to knowing and understanding the present and future. In telling the story of the Japanese American community an effective way of getting information is oral histories. Oral histories are the recording of interviews with people.

Adapted from information by Darcie Iki, Japanese American National Museum.

Interview someone in your family, like your grandfather or grandmother; they are a valuable source of knowledge and information about your family and the experience of Japanese Americans. Do it soon. You will learn a lot and you will feel closer to the person you interviewed.

Here are some hints for taking an oral history.
Find out everything about the person before you start. This will help you to prepare your questions and focus.

Make an outline of topics you want to cover.
Prepare your questions. Ask who, what, where, when, why, how, just like a good detective. Use open-ended questions, like "What do you remember about your father?" rather than "What was your father's name?"

You might want to ask the person you interview to bring along some old photos; it's a good stimulus for remembering stories.

Use a tape recorder.
Check it out before you begin your interview to make sure it is working properly and that the sound is at a good level.

Choose a quiet place for the interview where you will not be interrupted.

When you begin your interview ask your questions clearly; listen carefully. Ask follow-up questions. Try to get as many details as possible.

Check your machine to see it is working properly.

After you have finished, make sure to label your tape with the name of your subject and the date.

111

INTERVIEW with Grandma Mitsui
Oral History by Tani Mitsui Brown (March 1998)

My grandmother's name is Akiko Mitsui and she is the Grandma of me, Tani Mitsui Brown. "Aki" means autumn in the Japanese language and she was born in September, which is in the autumn season. The "ko" added on her name means "the daughter of."

Grandma was born in Montebello, California and moved to Puente, San Gabriel Valley, where her father farmed. She grew up during the Depression years, but she never realized it. She had a wonderful childhood back then, with many hills and valleys to explore. In those days, she says, more space was devoted to country land and trees.

Grandma attended school at Rowland Elementary School. She tells me that she was the class valedictorian (there were only twelve in her class!). She loved school and her favorite subjects were Reading, Spelling, History, and Social Studies. She had difficulty with Arithmetic though, and to this day, she says she is not an expert in adding and subtracting. But she loved to read.

My Grandma loved to read so much at school that the class prophecy predicted she would become a librarian. Little did anyone realize that she would work 24 years at Beverly Hills High School as a Library Assistant.

My Grandma is also an avid sports fan. She reads the sports page every day. She attends my cousin's Little League games and thinks I am a natural athlete.

I forgot to add how many there were in her family. There were eight kids and six are still alive. The oldest sister is now 92 and the youngest is 70. She is 75 and healthy, alert and still reading all the time.

I'm looking forward to spending Grandparents' Day with Grandma at my school this Spring.

Bibliography

Araki, Nancy and Jane M. Horii. *Matsuri: Festival Japanese American Celebrations and Activities.* Heian International, 1978.

Blyth, R.H. *Haiku.* San Francisco: The Hokuseido Press, 1982, vol. 3.

Centenary United Methodist Church. *Centenary Favorites.* Los Angeles: Centenary United Methodist Church, 1986.

Children's Museum, The. *A Japanese Idea Sheet.* Boston: The Children's Museum, 1985.

Downer, Lesley and Minoru Yoneda. *Step-By-Step Japanese Cooking.* New York: 1986.

Ekiguchi, Kunio and Ruth S. McCreery. *A Japanese Touch for the Seasons.* Tokyo: Kodansha International, 1987.

Ekiguchi, Kunio. *Creative Ideas from Japan.* Tokyo: Kodansha International, 1989.

Furuya, Kensho. *Kodo: Ancient Ways.* Santa Clarita: Ohara Publications, 1996.

Haslam, Andrew and Clare Doran. *Make it Work! Old Japan.* New York: Two-Can Publishing, 1995.

Hirasuna, Diane J. *Flavors of Japan.* San Francisco: 101 Productions, 1989.

Japanese American Cultural & Community Center. *Oshogatsu.* Los Angeles: JACCC, 1993.

Japanese American Cultural & Community Center. *Obon: A Gathering of Joy.* Los Angeles: JACCC, 1993.

Joya, Mock. *Things Japanese.* Tokyo: The Japan Times, 1985.

Kinnara Inc. *Horaku: A Celebration of Buddhist Performing Arts.* Los Angeles: Kinnara Inc., 1984.

Kodani, Masao. *Cocktails.* Los Angeles. Los Angeles: Senshin Buddhist Temple, 1992.

Kodani, Masao. *Dharma Chatter.* Los Angeles: Senshin Buddhist Temple, 1993.

Kodansha Encyclopedia of Japan. Kodansha Ltd., Tokyo: 1983, vols. 1, 3 & 4.

Kojima, Setsuko and Gene A. Crane. *A Dictionary of Japanese Culture.* Torrance: Heian International, 1987.

Little Tokyo Service Center. *The Four Seasons of Tofu.* Los Angeles: Little Tokyo Service Center, 1997.

Masuda, Tadashi. *The Design Heritage of Noren: Traditional Japanese Store-Front.* Tokyo: Graphic-sha Publishing Co., Ltd., 1989.

Mitsukuni and Sesoko Tsune. *Naorai Communion of the Table*. Tokyo: Cosmo Public Relations Corp., 1989.

Mori, Edie. *A Place to Play Buddhist Things*. Los Angeles: Southern District Special Projects, 1986.

Murakami, Hyoe and Edward G. Seidensticker, eds. *Guides to Japanese Culure*. Tokyo: Japan Culture Institute, 1977.

Nakano,Ichiro. *101 Favorite Songs Taught in Japanese Schools*. Tokyo: The Japan Times Ltd., 1983

Niiya, Brian, ed. *Japanese American History: An A-to-Z Reference from 1868 to the Present*. New York: Facts on File Inc., 1993.

Richie, Donald. *A Taste of Japan*. Tokyo: Kodansha Intl., 1985.

Sakata, Hideaki. *Origami*. Tokyo: Grapha-sha Ltd., 1985.

Shurtleff, William and Akiko Aoyagi. *The Book of Tofu*. Brookline: Autumn Press, 1975.

Takahama, Toshie. *Origami for Fun*. Tokyo: Shufunotomo Co., Ltd.,1984.

Statler, Oliver. *All Japan: The Catalogue of Everything Japanese*. New York: William Morrow & Co., 1984.

Tames, Richard and Sheila. *Country Topics, Japan*. London: Franklin Watts, 1994.

World Fellowship Committee of the Tokyo Young Women's Christian Association, The. *Japanese Etiquette, An Introduction*. Tokyo: Charles E. Tuttle, 1955.

Yamamoto, Yoshiki. *Aisho Kashu*. Tokyo: Kin'en-sha, 1983

Yamashita, Hiroshi John. *Haiku Images*. Los Angeles: Hiroshi John Yamashita, 1981.

Index

Note: *An honorific prefix i.e., "o" and "go" often precede a noun, for example, ozōni and gohan. In conversation, a word will be used almost exclusively with the honorific, i.e., ohashi, omiyage, so that many primarily English-speaking Japanese Americans do not recognize or separate the base word from the honorific prefix. In the Index, words are listed without the honorific prefix, and cross-referenced with the prefix if the word is customarily used with the honorific prefix.*

aikidō 85-86
animal zodiac (Chinese astrological signs) 40-41, 110

Bon or Obon
  Obon 69-72
  bon odori 69-71
  Obon attire 69-70, 72
bow; how to 51
Boy's Day or Tango no Sekku 57
  koinobori or carp streamer 57-58,
  kabuto 64 See also Children's Day
Buddhism
  daruma 39
  enryo 108-109
  maneki neko 84

mottainai 105
namuamidabutsu 71
Obon 69-72
tsukemono 107

celebrations See festivals
chanto – (to be thorough and proper) 54-55
Children's Day or Kodomo-no-hi 57
  See also Boy's Day
chōchin 69, 74-75
clothing
  geta 70-72
  Obon attire 69-70
  happi 69
  kimono 46, 49-50
  yukata 49, 70, 72
  zori 72
counting in Japanese 24

daruma 39

enryo or to show restraint 108-109
  See also Buddhism
expressions in Japanese
  chotto-matte 70
  gochisōsama, 28
  itadakimasu 28
  omedetō 20
  onegai shimasu 70

118

festivals or celebrations
    Girl's Day or Hinamatsuri 45-47
    Obon 69-72
    Oshōgatsu 19-21
    Tanabata or Hoshimatsuri (Star Festival) 93
fish-printing or gyotaku 59
food
    carnival food 81
    chazuke 101
    eating Japanese food 32
    grandma's meal 99-101
    musubi 88-89
    mochi 34-35
    mochigashi or manjū 82-83
    musubi or nigiri 88-89
    osechi ryōri (New Year food) 21, 29-31
    ozōni 30
    sushi 15, 21
    tōfu 101, 104
    tsukemono 107
    winter foods 31
furoshiki 45, 76

Generations of Japanese Americans 23
    Issei 15, 20, 23-24, 26-27
    Nisei 15, 24
    Sansei 15, 24
    Yonsei 15, 24

gift or miyage 90
making gift wrap 90, 91
Girl's Day or Hinamatsuri 45-47
    making a hina doll 48
good-luck symbols
    daruma 39
    kame 38
    maneki neko 84
    tsuru 37
grandmother or bāchan (or obāchan) 15
    poem 26-27
    grandparent's house 98-101
    interview with Grandma Mitsui 112
gyotaku – See fish-printing 59

haiku 94-95
hashi or chopsticks 33
Jan-ken-pon 65
kanreki 100, 110
kimono, 46, 49; designing a kimono, 50
kitchen items 106

maneki neko 84
meal – Japanese meal 32
    Bāchan's rules 32-33
    eating with hashi (chopsticks) 33
miyage or gift 90
mochitsuki 34

Momotarō, Story of, 60-62; making Momotarō
  stick puppets 62-63
mottainai – to be wasteful 105
musubi 88-89 – See also nigiri

Nikkei – of Japanese heritage 15
Nisei Week JapaneseFestival 80
nigiri 88-89 – See also musubi
noren 102-103
numbers; writing in Japanese 24-25

obāchan – See grandmother
oral history how to 111-112
omiyage – See miyage
origami – art of paper folding
  making a hina doll 48
  kabuto 64
  kame 38
  tsuru 37
Oshōgatsu – See Shogatsu

Sakura or cherry blossoms 52,
  "Sakura," the song 52
  making a sakura decoration 53
senbazuru or 1,000 cranes 36
sensei or teacher 85-86, 110
Shōgatsu 19-21
  animal zodiac 40-41
  good-luck charms 36, (tsuru) 37, (kame) 38,
  (daruma) 39

Issei Oshōgatsu 20
mochi 34-35
mochitsuki 34
okasane 19
osechi ryōri (New Year Foods) 20-21, 29-30, 31
ozōni recipe 30
Symbols 19
okasane or kagami-mochi 19
tsuru 37
Star Festival or Hoshimatsuri 93

Tanabata See Star Festival
Tankō Bushi (Japanese folk song) 73
tōfu 104
taiko – drum 71-72, 77
  making a taiko 78, 79

wrapping paper 90-91
zodiac – See Animal zodiac

120

Acknowledgements and Thank yous

Project Director & Writer Chris Aihara

Art Direction & Design Qris Yamashita

Illustration Glen Iwasaki

Cover Photography Ed Ikuta
Cover Composition Russell Oshita
Cover Models Kisa Ito, Hannah Komai, *and* Keisho Maehara

Inside Photography Individually Credited
Ed Ikuta
Hirokazu Kosaka
Keith Nakata
Bill Ross
Steve Sakai

Kanji Hirokazu Kosaka

Contributing Writers
Lucy Asako Boltz
Mary Jane Tomi Boltz
Tani Mitsui Brown
Naomi Hirahara
Rev. Masao Kodani
Marion Manaka
Joyce Nako
Daisy Nakai
Michiko Tagawa
Rev. H. John Yamashita

Edward Asawa
Reiko Bissey
Jane Boltz
Marcie Chan
Dyer-Mutchnick Group
Franklin D. Murphy Library
Rev. Kensho Furuya
Frances Hashimoto & Mikawaya
Yoshi Honkawa
Darcie Iki
Sandra & Lillian Ikuta
Meg Imamoto
Lloyd Inui
Tazuko Inui
Janet Ito
Leslie Ito
Rev. Noriaki Ito
Japanese American National Museum
Gary Kawaguchi
Hal Keimi
Brian Kito & Fugetsudo
Shirley Kodani
Kats Kunitsugu
Kiyokane Families & Rascal's
Chris Komai
Kayce Komai
Gail Kuida
Linda Machida
Aki & Masao Maehara

Mas Matsumoto
Ellen Minami
Janet Mitsui Brown
Akira Miyazaki
Toyo Miyatake Studio
Johnny Mori
Carolyn Morinishi & *The KaMai Forum*
Lori Nakama
The Rafu Shimpo
Jill Ruby
Jo Sayama
Senshin Buddhist Temple
Joyce Shimazu
Bill Shishima
Yuki Tanaka
Chiyo Takemoto
Carol Tanita & Rafu Bussan
Iris Teragawa
Laura Tokunaga
Minoru & Mary Tonai
Teresa Tonai
JoAnn Yamada
Richard Yamashita
Sandra Yamate & Polychrome Publishing
Gerald D. Yoshitomi

Thank you to Mrs. Iori Yachi, Consulate General of Japan in Los Angeles

121

ABOUT THE Japanese American Cultural & Community Center

Located in the downtown Los Angeles area known as "Little Tokyo," the Japanese American Cultural & Community Center (JACCC) is a cultural and community organization dedicated to the presentation and promotion of Japanese and Japanese American cultural arts. The completion of the JACCC was the dream of visionary Issei and Nisei (first and second generation) Japanese American pioneers who wanted to create a permanent center for the community and its future generations. Completed in phases from 1980-83, the facility includes the five-story Center Building housing the museum-quality George J. Doizaki Gallery, conference room facilities, the award-winning James Irvine Japanese Garden, and the Plaza designed by Isamu Noguchi. The 880-seat Japan America Theatre adjacent to the Center Building is the venue for presentations ranging from performances of Grand Kabuki to contemporary work by Japanese American artists.

Japanese American Cultural & Community Center
244 S. San Pedro Street, Suite 505
Los Angeles, CA 90012
Telephone: 213/628-2725
Fax: 213/617-8576
E-mail: jaccc@anet.net
http://koma.org/apa/jaccc

123

Other Books from Polychrome Publishing

Almond Cookies & Dragon Well Tea
ISBN #1-879965-03-8
by Cynthia Chin-Lee; illustrations by You Shan Tang.
Erica, an European American girl, visits the home of Nancy, her Chinese American friend and finds much to admire and enjoy. In introducing her friend to her family's culture, Nancy discovers that she needn't feel embarrassed or ashamed about it. "Well crafted. Very stylish for today's America." *The Book Reader.*

Ashok By Any Other Name   ISBN #1-879965-01-1
by Sandra S. Yamate; illustrations by Janice Tohinaka.
Ashok, an Indian American boy who wishes he had a more "American" name searches for the perfect name for himself. A story for every immigrant or child of immigrants who struggles to be an American. "The book is well-written and would make an excellent addition to a primary school library." *India West.*

Blue Jay In The Desert   ISBN #1-879965-04-6
by Marlene Shigekawa; illustrations by Isao Kikuchi
A Japanese American boy and his family are interned during World War II. A good introduction for children to the history of the Japanese American internment.

Children of Asian America   ISBN #1-879965-15-1
compiled on behalf of the Asian American Coalition.
An anthology about the experiences of Asian American children from eleven different Asian ethnic communities: Bangladeshi, Cambodian, Chinese, Filipino, Indian, Japanese, Korean, Laotian, Pakistani, Thai, Vietnamese, plus bi-racial and pan-Asian American. "[This] book can help all of us deal with the complex identity of being Asian American., . . . an engaging piece of literature, punctuated throughout with captivating photos." *Northwest Asian Weekly.*

Chopsticks From America   ISBN #1-879965-11-9
by Elaine Hosozawa-Nagano; illustrations by Masayuki Miyata.
When two children move to Japan, they learn that life in Japan is not what they expected. But before long the unfamiliar becomes familiar and the familiar expands to encompass tolerance and acceptance of that which is different. A Parent Council Choice Book. Recommended by the *Children's Book Review* and *Midwest Bookwatch.*

The Lobster and The Sea   ISBN #1-879965-14-3
by Esther Chiu; illustrations by Mika Takahashi.
An Asian American child must reconcile American values with Asian ones when Grandfather decides it is time to return Home. This tale will reassure any child faced with the imminent departure of a grandparent or other loved one that separation will not undermine the infinite nature of love.

One Small Girl   ISBN #1-879965-05-4
by Jennifer L. Chan; illustrations by Wendy K. Lee.
Jennifer Lee is one small girl trying to amuse herself in Grandmoth-er's store and Uncle's store next door. A rhythmic and whimsical tale about a small girl's fun fooling big grown-ups. "Kids will delight in the sound effects of shoes clicking on store floors and a small girl's discovery of personal power." *Children's Bookwatch.*

Stella: On The Edge Of Popularity   ISBN #1-879965-08-9
by Lauren Lee.
Stella, a Korean American pre-teen, is caught between two cultures. At home, Grandmother insists that Stella be a good Korean girl, but at school, Stella is American, aching to be popular and fit in. "Well-developed characters and a credible plot will hold the interest of readers." *School Library Journal.* "A must-read for parents and their children." *Korea Central Daily News.*

Thanksgiving At Obaachan's   ISBN #1-879965-07-0
by Janet Mitsui Brown.
A Japanese American girl explains why her Grandmother makes Thanksgiving so special. Anyone whose family has expanded this American holiday to include reminders of their cultural heritage will appreciate this little girl's Thanksgiving and treasure the memories it evokes. Named Pick of the Lists and a Parent Council Selection. "Warm, intergenerational and reminiscent of life with grandmother . . . a family story, beautifully illustrated, lovingly told." *American Bookseller.* "The quintessential Sansei story." *San Francisco Examiner.*